Sherwood Memories

A History of Sherwood Township Clark County, Wisconsin

Kay Moeller Scholtz

Cover Photo – Hunters at Sherwood, Circa 1900 (Pickering Family Photo)
L to R: David Sparks, brothers David, Earl, & Myron Pickering

Order online at Amazon.com

ISBN: 978-1-50865-456-8 First Edition

Copyright © 2015   Kay Scholtz

Contents

Author's Note

Sherwood Beginnings *1*

Early Settlers *3*

Indian Encampments *13*

Schools *15*

Waterways *21*

La Flesh Family Stories *23*

Buffalo Bill's Visit *29*

Boom Times – 1880s *33*

Perkins Family Stories *35*

Myron Pickering & the Bear Trapper *39*

Myron's Memoirs *47*

Post Offices *59*

Early 1900s *61*

Businesses *67*

Churches *75*

Sherwood Cemetery *79*

Fun Times in Early Days *83*

The Depression *87*

Sherwood Lake – A Grand Idea! *93*

War Time – How We Coped *99*

Post World War II *103*

Deer Hunting – A Way of Life *107*

Real Characters *113*

Recent Times *121*

Credits *123*

The Point at Sherwood Lake – (Jennifer Shirk Photo)

Author's Note

Established in 1874, the Town of Sherwood is located in the southeast corner of Clark County, Wisconsin. Sherwood Township evolved from a wilderness in the mid-1800s, to a farming community by the early 1900s. The township's rich history includes memories of frequent visits from Wisconsin Governor Cadwallader C. Washburn in the 1880s and Buffalo Bill with his hunting party in 1886.

The creation of Sherwood Lake in the 1930s is also a special part of the town's history. The sad state of the lake, after a failure of the auxiliary spillway in February of 2014 and structural problems with the dam, has prompted me to write this history today. With strong group efforts we will see the lake restored soon.

Through over 140 years of change in landscape and residents, Sherwood continues to be a place to relax and enjoy nature.

I'd like to give special thanks to all who have shared information about their families and photos with me to help tell Sherwood's story. For anything I've unintentionally left out in the pages ahead, perhaps another history can be written at a later date by another friend of Sherwood.

With shared memories of the more recent past to recollections from those who walked the land more than one hundred years before us, I'd like this book to be a small souvenir to all of you from a place that I have called home most of my life, a place that has brought a sense of peacefulness and beauty to so many.

Kay Scholtz

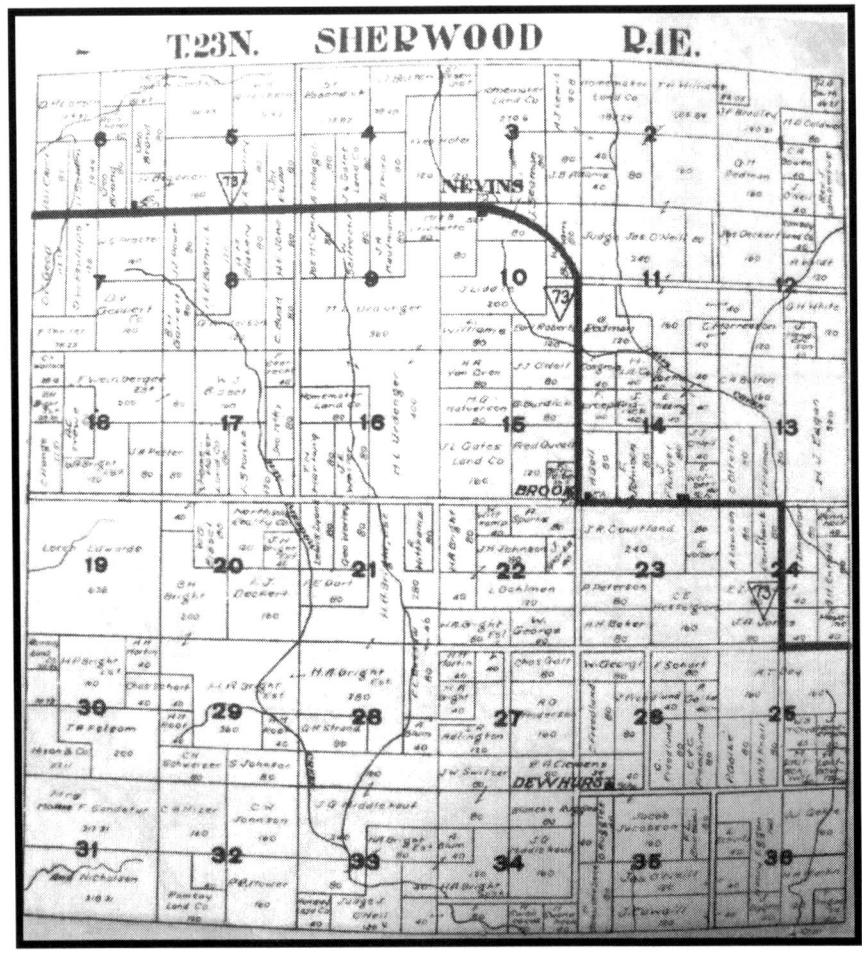

Plat of Sherwood Township from 1906
(For reference to locations of Sections mentioned in the text)

Sherwood Beginnings

A wilderness we now call Town of Sherwood, in central Wisconsin, first heard white man's footsteps not long after surveyors blazed the trees and marked the section corners in the 1850s. Abundant mighty white pines growing along the little creeks towered over the landscape. One can only imagine the whispers they made when breezes blew through them and the dollar signs envisioned by the lumber cruisers who first gazed upon them. Those large white pine trees are what brought settlers to this area in search of fortune. They are what began the taming of Sherwood Forest, a yet unnamed township in Clark County, Wisconsin.

Washburn Township, created in 1873 with 72 sections, contained land that one year later became a new township when settlers in the eastern half chose to separate. This left Washburn, and the newly created township, each with the standard 36 sections. The first chairman of the new township was William W. La Flesh, a Wisconsin Civil War veteran. The name chosen for the township, Perkins, was presumably after Daniel Perkins, one of the town's oldest settlers and a respected Civil War veteran himself. Perkins owned land in Section 34 near the present day Sherwood County Park.

Two years later, in 1876, a petition was circulated in the township and presented to the Clark County Board, to change the name from Perkins to Sherwood Forest. Why Sherwood Forest? I believe it was by suggestion of Elizabeth La Flesh, as the wilderness she encountered reminded her of Sherwood Forest, the Royal Forest near Nottinghamshire, England. Elizabeth was born in England and apparently the town board members liked the name including her husband, Tom, who served as town chairman for the next six years.

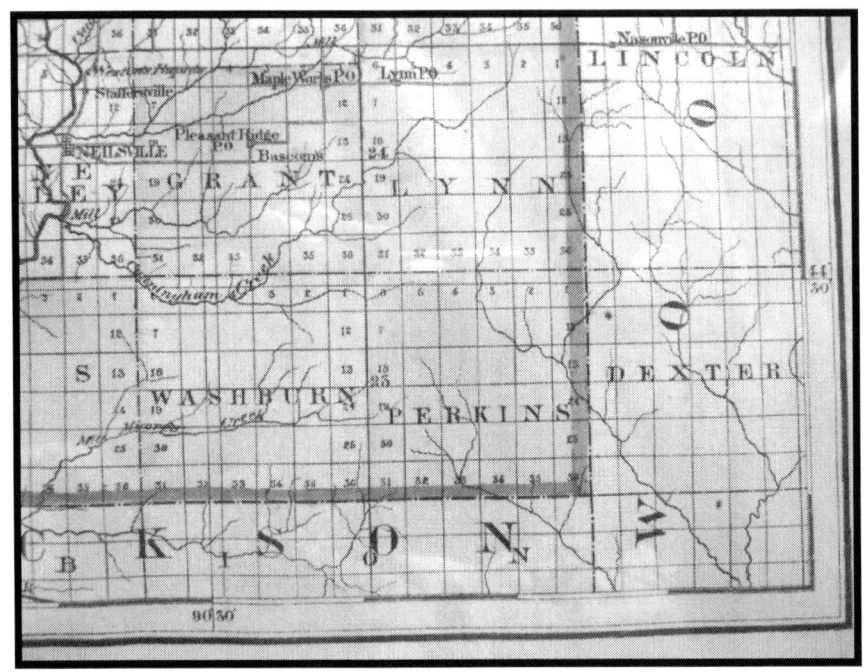

Page from an Atlas by H. F. Walling © 1876
(Author's collection)

Regarding the name change from Perkins to Sherwood Forest, Hugh Perkins wrote a letter to a friend in the 1880s and told him the town's name was changed due to "politics". The name, Perkins, was dropped ten years before Hugh and his brother, Miner, got into their own pickles. One can speculate that the Perkins brothers rubbed their neighbors the wrong way early on in Sherwood. I'll mention later the troubles Hugh and Miner Perkins found themselves involved with in the 1880s.

In 1900, the Sherwood town board circulated a second petition to change the name of the town again from Sherwood Forest to simply Sherwood. The board had the notion that the "Forest" part gave prospective settlers the impression that land in Sherwood Township was not good for farming. Clark County agreed to the name change and the word "Forest" was gone for good. At this time, in 1900, most of the white pine logging was finished in Sherwood. Hardwood sawmills popped up here and there and disappeared when the mature hardwood trees did.

Early Settlers

McDonald's Logging Crew on the Tote Road between Sherwood and City Point Circa 1891 - From a stereo card by Photographer M. Kelly

Lumbermen from the La Crosse, Wisconsin, area led the way to this beautiful location. One in particular, Cadwallader Colden Washburn (namesake of Washburn Township), future governor of Wisconsin, had the money and ambition to turn those tall white pine trees into lumber. He purchased thousands of acres of wilderness in Clark County and surrounding areas of central Wisconsin in the 1860s and 1870s. C. C. Washburn, as he was most often called, hired Thomas Jefferson La Flesh to set up a lumber camp in Sherwood Forest in about 1869. Through the next decade, La Flesh took charge of hiring and running several logging camps for Washburn who backed him financially. The two men had met previously during the start of the Civil War, in La Crosse, when Washburn organized Company B, of the 2nd Wisconsin Cavalry and named La Flesh as a 1st Lieutenant of the Company. La Flesh, a young and brilliant soldier, was married in 1862 to Elizabeth Summerside at Black Earth, Wisconsin, and came out of the Civil War with a Captain's rank.

Along with C. C. Washburn, other lumbermen purchased acreage throughout the township creating employment for those earliest Sherwood Forest settlers. A large group of pioneers, many related to one another and originating from Sullivan County, New York, moved to Sherwood Forest from Plainfield, Waushara County, Wisconsin, in the 1870s. Some of their surnames were Sparks, Pickering, Meddaugh, Doughty, and Perkins. These farm families, true pioneers, dived into cutting timber, grubbed out stumps, and worked hard to make their dreams come true. In wintertime they worked at logging to supplement their farm income. Without money earned from logging they wouldn't have been able to start building their homesteads. Lumbering and farming went hand in hand and became a way of life for these earliest settlers.

Peter McGinnis came to the area in 1872 when he purchased 120 acres in Section 8 of the yet to be, Town of Perkins. Peter was born in New York. Before locating in this area, he traveled to California and back twice, during the gold rush days. McGinnis reflected on his memories of those early days in Sherwood in the *Neillsville Republican Press* in December of 1910. "There were some settlers in the town of Sherwood a few years before me. One of these was Mr. Benedict who was a near neighbor when I first got there. Also a Mr. Coudrey [Town Chairman in 1875]. I can't really say but it was thirty-nine or forty years ago that we got in there. It was on Christmas day. Yes, well I might go on and tell the story, how it happened. I got a man to load up our stuff when we started up here and in getting the stove he lost the back of it and we did not miss it until we got out to Benedict's and we had to remain there a whole week until I got back to La Crosse to get it. I was toting so I brought it back when I brought up a load. At that time my wife was suffering with a bad felon on her hand, piled up, as you might say, with ten children. Then I got into my own house. Well, then, I started to go to work and worked a week with my team and the man had a friend whom he thought more of than he did of me and he discharged me. So I left my team and went to work with my hands. I worked a week and was taken sick." "Let's see, then I went back to work in a camp and stayed there until the camp broke up after which I went on a drive, a job that I had never done before. All this time I did not like this place but I had no money to get out. This was my first winter in Clark County." Peter McGinnis left his Sherwood farm in 1904, settling in Neillsville where he died in 1914.

The Sherwood Sparks family settlers consisted of several brothers, Thomas, John, James, Robert, Jesse, and their father, James Freeman Sparks. They followed the path, like several others, from Sullivan County, New York, to Waushara County, Wisconsin, and then to Sherwood in the 1870s. Their sister, Hannah, wife of Byron Pickering, settled in the north half of the township. Byron lived on Tom's Creek, first in Section 10, south of Thomas La Flesh's Ranch, and later purchased the ranch for his family.

James Freeman Sparks - Patriarch of the Sparks Family
(Fields Collection)

L to R Back: **David St. Germain, Robert Sparks**
L to R Front: **Thomas Sparks, Jesse Sparks**
(Fields Collection)

Sparks siblings married into the Messing, Lawson, Ellis, and St. Germain families of Sherwood and together they made up a large portion of Sherwood's early settlers. James Freeman Sparks, a widower in his sixties, came to live in Sherwood in 1878 and took turns living with his married children throughout the township. His great grandson, M. Ward Wilson, shared this about his grandfather, "J. F. Sparks, known as Grandpa Sparks to Sherwood Forest folks, was a loveable and colorful character. Although he called home the house and family of his daughter Elizabeth [St. Germain], he also frequently visited daughter, Hannah [Pickering], four sons, and other relatives in the community. It was not unusual to see him trudging along the dusty road carrying a carpet bag valise, containing a few personal belongings plus a supply of "Grand-dad's liniment", some pills and salve, which he would sell along the way, thus obtaining some spending money." James F. Sparks died at his daughter, Elizabeth's home in Section 8.

Jesse, Thomas, John, and Elizabeth (St. Germain) Sparks chose to live out their lives in Sherwood and all are buried at Sherwood Cemetery. A few Sparks siblings moved to western states.

A Civil War veteran buried in Sherwood Cemetery, David St. Germain, had a very interesting and tragic family background. David married Sarah Elizabeth (Sparks) later in life, a second marriage for both of them. He and Sarah lived in Section 8. David's mother, Theresa Gagnier, lost her first husband near Prairie du Chein at the same time her infant daughter was scalped, when the family was attacked at their farm home by a Winnebago chief named Red Bird and his four companions in 1827. There were conflicts at this time between different Native American tribes and white settlers drawn to this area by the lead mining boom. Theresa, and her infant daughter who survived the attack, were later awarded property for their suffering and loss. Theresa Gagnier later remarried Guilliame William St. Germain and they had two more children, David, who settled in Sherwood, and Hattie.

David's son, Mose St. Germain, from his first marriage, was the father of Hazel St. Germain Grange, wife of Wallace Grange. Hazel and Wallace Grange founded the Sand Hill Wildlife Game Farm west of Babcock, Wisconsin. Upon retiring the Grange's sold their farm, consisting of over nine thousand acres, to the state of Wisconsin with the stipulation that the land be used for wildlife education as it still is today.

David wrote to his son Gabriel from his home at Nevins in 1888. Below is a portion of a letter shared with me by Gabriel's great grandson.

Nevins, Wis, May 20, 1888
Dear Son, I received your letter some time ago, was glad to hear from you... La Flesh sold everything in here at Sheriff Sale. Byron Pickering got 5 forties and all the buildings, store and all, for a $1000.

.. Albert Sholtz lives where he did. There has not been any great change there. He got 6 forties for $125.
Mr. Boyington from Pittsville got the mill and all that was around it for $725. They are going to build two miles of railroad from Newtown on toward Mapleworks [near Granton] this summer.
David [Sarah's son David Sparks who was David St. Germain's stepson and lived with them] bought 7 calves last fall for $19.50 so we have eleven calves and 17 sheep and 4 cows... David has been on the drive [logging drive] all spring. My wife is not very well, she has the sick headache. Wish you could come and see us as soon as you can and wish you would send us your picture if you please... My wife and me send our love I remain your father. D. St. Germain

In the north half of Sherwood, in Section 9, a large saw mill was purchased and most likely upgraded by Pittsville businessmen who called their business the Wood County Manufacturing Company. The mill cut mostly white and red oak logs into lumber, staves for barrels, etc. Many men worked there and this was the mill David St. Germain referred to in the above letter to his son Gabriel.

Albert Scholtz, another early settler mentioned in David's letter, came to Sherwood Forest by 1876 and worked for a time for Tom La Flesh at logging and also farmed later. Albert bought land from the C. C. Washburn estate in the north half of Sherwood and built a farm there in the 1880s. He married Bertha Zipfel from Town of Grant in 1880. Albert contracted out a few logging jobs on his own but had limited success. Scholtz traveled to La Crosse in the summer of 1893 to find help for some medical problems he was having. His family got word two weeks later that he'd been found dead in the basement of the European Hotel there. The press said he died of brain fever, leaving behind Bertha and their five children, with another one on the way. Bertha managed to keep the farm, raise all her children, and marry twice more to husbands who both left her, but blessed her with three more children. Bertha took in extra income by cooking for the sawmill crew of the Wood County Manufacturing Company as she lived next door. She also boarded some of the millworkers and passersby in her large home. Her son, Ralph Scholtz, took over the farm and married a neighbor girl, Clara Gall. Together, Ralph and Clara raised four children and lived out their lives in Sherwood.

South of Sherwood Forest was the township of Sullivan, later named City Point. Sullivan was a busy place with a shingle mill town next door to the east in Wood County called Scranton that sat along the East Fork of the Black River and the railroad tracks. Several Sherwood land owners found work at City Point around 1880 including Scholtz, Meddaugh, and McCormick. John L. Sullivan, a Civil War veteran, was the namesake of the township. He moved to Sherwood for several years but later returned to City Point where he died. J. L. Sullivan was active in lumbering and politics, serving on both the Clark and Jackson County boards, and also dabbled in real estate. At one time he owned a farm on Sherwood's south side and ran a mill there in the 1880s. His ex-wife kept another farm they owned north of Sherwood Lake, for a short time, after she and John divorced.

John L. Sullivan later married Kitty Meddaugh, who grew up near the Dewhurst school house in Sherwood. A famous boxer who was the first heavyweight champion, shared the same name as John L. Sullivan. John got a kick out of people thinking he might be the boxer.

Jacob & Annette (Jensen) Jacobson – (Jacobson Family Photo)

Another early settler who came from City Point to Sherwood Forest was Jacob Jacobson. He logged, farmed, and was active in town politics and on the school board. The Dewhurst School was located next to his Sherwood farm. Jacob immigrated from Norway as did his future bride, Annette, and they were married at Spaulding, Jackson County, Wisconsin, in May of 1890. Before coming to America, Jacob was a concert violinist in Trygstad, Norway. In his early days at Sherwood he walked to a lumber camp at 4 a.m. every morning where he was employed as camp cook, about two miles from his farm. The camp was located where Sherwood Park is today. Jacob played the fiddle at the lumber camp, for dances, and at home with accompaniment by his family. Jacob and Annette Jacobson chose to live out their lives in Sherwood and have many descendants still living in the township.

Stillman Ellis purchased land near the center of Sherwood in Section 14. In 1879 he owned seven oxen, three wagons, carriages, and sleighs, and had the largest number of cattle in Sherwood. Stillman was town chairman from 1886 to 1888. The property for the Sherwood Town Hall was sold to the township by Stillman. His first wife, Henrietta Ellis, has one of the earliest gravestones in the Sherwood Cemetery. Her remains were moved from the Ellis property (now owned by the Moeller family) to the cemetery many years after her death, in 1898, along with her son, Charles, and daughter, Susan Ellis Hammond. The town board hired Joseph Janes, Stillman's son-in-law, to move the remains. Stillman moved to Portage County, Wisconsin, when elderly. He died there at Bancroft in 1919. Stillman's daughter, Bloomy, married Thomas Sparks, and his daughter Henrietta married Joseph Janes, all buried in Sherwood Cemetery.

Joseph Janes carved out a farm in Section 24, arriving in Sherwood in 1874 where he purchased 120 acres. He and wife, Henrietta Ellis, had five children. Joseph was a civil war veteran, and drove a "stage" line delivering mail from Shortville to Nevins for many years. His "stage" consisted of a single seated lightweight wagon pulled by horse in summertime and a sleigh drawn by a very nice team of horses in wintertime, according to a descendant, Charles H. Clark. Mail was transported two or three times weekly.

The last member of the Janes family to live in Sherwood was youngest daughter, Flora, who never married. She was a kind soul who lived on her farm with cousin, Jess Sparks, after both her parents passed.

Family stories were that a boyfriend she loved was not good enough for her parents. Flora loved to bake and she babysat neighbor children.

Several other families lived in the Janes home after Flora passed, and later it was moved from Sherwood to a location on the west side of Hwy 13 just northwest of Pinecrest Supper Club and remains there to this day.

Although identity is uncertain, I believe this to be a photo of Joseph Janes, Sherwood mail carrier. Another photo of the same man with a pair of horses and the same buggy shows up in the Pickering Family photo collection. (Scholtz Family Photo)

Andrew Lawson was another of Sherwood's earliest pioneer farmers. He was born in Denmark in 1849 and came to America with his brother Sam, working in Greenland for a time in soda mines. In 1872 he came to Wisconsin, and in the mid-1870s he began working at a saw mill in the Sherwood area, purchasing his future farm and homestead in Section 24. He married Ascenith Sparks and they began their married life with only an ox team and no milk cows. Andrew walked to City Point, 11 miles, to buy flour and groceries and carried them home on his back. He also walked to Neillsville when he needed supplies and thought little of it. The first Lawson home was a log home as were most of the early settlers. Andrew and Ascenith's only son, Ralph, took over the farm along with his wife Nettie. They had two sons, Howard (who died when a young boy), and Arlo Lawson.

Indian Encampments

Early settlers blended with Indians passing through Sherwood Forest who didn't feel a need to settle permanently at any one location. Natives, most likely Winnebago and now known as Ho Chunk, were used to traveling from season to season and carrying their makeshift shelters with them wherever they roamed. In blueberry season they located where fruit could be harvested and did the same during cranberry season. They had annual routines for harvesting game, wild fruit, mushrooms, and herbs, patterns no doubt handed down for generations.

Byron Pickering's grandson, M. Ward Wilson said the Indians were friendly and traveled in small groups. One time Wilson recalled how a group helped save Byron's horse when it was stuck in a Sherwood swamp.

Sherwood settlers recalled teepees popping up here and there between their homesteads from time to time. A young boy named Ralph Scholtz, who lived in the north half of Sherwood Township, remembered walking across the road from his farm to satisfy his curiosity when a group of Indians appeared there one day putting up their shelters in the late 1890s. When he approached a newly erected teepee, Ralph pulled open the flap to see several women seated on the floor. They were covered in smoke and laughed at him. It was a memory the young boy would never forget.

A school teacher who taught at Sherwood Forest, Maud Safford, was invited to visit an Indian chief who had recently set up camp in the southern part of the township in 1887. Miss Safford wrote about her experience briefly and described what she saw on a December evening in a local newspaper interview. There were about a dozen "tents" as she called them, set up together, with a soft glow of light inside each one. The tents were warm inside and snug, and the chief whom she visited was busy making molded bullets for his son. He sat cross legged on a matt in front of his fire. The chief asked Maud if she would be interested in letting his son, who had previous schooling in

Black River Falls, attend her one room school nearby. She told him she wouldn't mind, if the school board would allow her to. He had requested that she come to visit with him that evening, his son's schooling was the reason.

Maud heard mothers singing softly to their children while visiting the native encampment in the darkness. She saw a young child strapped to a cradle board whose mother entertained him by shaking beads attached to the top of it. The mother was sewing up a pair of moccasins. Teenaged boys rode away from the little village on their ponies, wrapped in red colored blankets and wearing red caps, their long black hair flowing behind them. It looked as though they were out for an evening joy ride.

Maud felt an appreciation for the carefree lifestyle the natives seemed to have and thought it was an inviting way to live. The Indians were visiting Sherwood then to harvest venison. They were successful and Maud noticed large pieces of the dried meat hung from poles supporting the tent, being smoked. She only learned one of their names, White Dog, a young man with a wife and six month old infant whom she spoke with in a neighboring tent.

Maud also was entertained by a young boy who danced for her and then whipped out a hat, hoping to collect a tip. A Sherwood resident who she referred to as Mr. S., who had driven her to the campsite, dropped a coin in the child's hat.

As they rode away into the darkness to the north that evening in Mr. S's cutter, Maud looked back at the tents and saw glowing lights illuminate through each one of them. It was an evening the young school teacher would never forget. Her story gives us a glimpse into what the Indian encampment at Sherwood looked like.

The Indian settlement continued from season to season for many years, just northwest of the corner of now Ballard Road and County Trunk Z.

Schools

The school that Maud Safford taught at was called Birdland Echo School. It was located in the east central part of the township in Section 14. At one time there were four schools in Sherwood; Birdland Echo, Audubon, Longfellow, and Dewhurst. School houses were built about every two miles so children wouldn't have too far to walk.

Longfellow School was located near the northwest end of the township in Section 6. Longfellow was built in 1902. It was not used for too many years as there were not enough students in that area, some walked there from the Town of Washburn. The land the school house was sitting on was sold to Oscar Brinkmeier in the 1930s. After being empty for a number of years, Oscar moved the school to his farm in Section 4, and used it for a shed. Longfellow was probably the smallest school house in Sherwood.

Birdland Echo School was located one half mile east of the town hall. Esther Sharp Dodte taught school at Birdland Echo in 1929. I had a chance to talk with her when she was in her 90s and learned that she taught my father, aunt, and uncle at Birdland and remembered all of them. Esther said she boarded at the Albert Gall home just northwest of the school around the curve on Highway 73. She had never hunted before but during deer season that year the Gall's handed her a gun.

Mrs. Dodte said she enjoyed her teaching days at Sherwood but walking from Galls to school was sometimes difficult. In springtime she would take off her shoes and carry them as the roads were so muddy and she didn't want to ruin her foot ware. Esther said she caught rides home to Neillsville with the milk man during school vacations. When Birdland Echo closed, the building was sold to someone from Granton and moved there to be used as a garage next to a residence.

Teachers were paid a monthly salary and in addition to teaching they were expected to fire up the woodstoves in the school rooms early each morning and keep them clean. Nearby residents placed bids with the local school board hoping to get the chance to sell firewood and kindling to the schools each year. Pine stumps left behind from the logging days were chopped up in bundles and made excellent wood for starting fires.

Teachers were also expected to provide a good quality program for the entire neighborhood to attend at the end of the school year, especially in those early days.

Many early Sherwood teachers ended up marrying sons of the families they boarded with. In the Byron Pickering family, three sons married Sherwood school teachers. Maud Safford came to Sherwood from Neillsville and boarded with the La Flesh family but she went back home single as did Esther Sharp.

Dewhurst School was located in the south half of Sherwood in Section 26. It closed in about 1945 and children were then transported to Audubon. About this time a school bus route began and several Sherwood residents drove the route until Audubon's closure. Some bus drivers were Oscar Brinkmeier, Joe Rosandich, Wilbur Fields, and Chester Freedlund.

Hattie (Sparks) & Reuben Fields – Sherwood School Bus
Circa 1950 (Fields Family Photo)

When Dewhurst School closed, the building was sold to Al Cramer who moved it to his land on the south edge of Sherwood near the Clark/Jackson County line. He and wife, Lydia, used it for their residence for many years. Before the building was recently torn down, a large homemade blackboard was found in the attic with Jacob Jacobson's signature on it written with chalk, with a 1890s date.

At least two of Sherwood's school houses were first built of logs. The original log school house on the Scholtz property near the present Audubon school burned down in the early 1890s and was rebuilt shortly afterward where it is located yet today. Audubon is the only school house in Sherwood still standing and is used as a family hunting and gathering place. It was the last school to operate in Sherwood and closed in 1963.

Birdland Echo School – Gertrude E. Walport, Teacher – Circa 1913
Back Row L to R: Miss Walport, ?, Hazel Sparks, ?, Ralph Lawson (tall with cap), Lillian (Ziemendorf) Klebnow, Charles Clark, Helen Sparks, ?, ?, ?, Ada (Ziemendorf) Zuelsdorf. Front Row L to R: ?, ?, Daniel Sparks, Bessie Coulthard, , ?, ?, Margie Coulthard, Roy Hill, Lucille (Ziemendorf) Stuebs, Joe Hill, ? , ?. (Postcard from the Fields Photo Collection)

Birdland Echo School in the Mid-1930s - Back Row L to R: Leo Coulthard, George Florence, Teacher - Frieda Kurtz, Roseyln Messing, Loretta Fluegel, Theresa Moeller. Front Row L to R: Betty Florence, Ardo Fluegel, Allen Rennhack, Axel Moeller

Audubon School – Built in 1891, now owned by the Rosandick family

Dewhurst School –Located in Section 26.
Sold to Al Cramer in the 1950s and used as his residence.

Birdland Echo school house being moved to Granton after it was sold. This photo was taken from Ardo Fluegel's driveway on Hwy 73 as the truck was heading west.　　(Fluegel Family Photo)

Waterways

Several creeks wind their way through Sherwood Township. All of them flow into the East Fork of the Black River and then to the main Black River that makes its way to Onalaska and La Crosse. Hay Meadow Creek, now shortened in name to Hay Creek, is a small creek that starts on the west side of the township and runs down through the southeast corner. Upon entering neighboring Jackson County, Hay Creek flows into the East Fork of the Black. Lumberman built at least three dams on Hay Meadow Creek pre1900. One of those dams was located in Section 34. It was a large dam that backed up a huge amount of marsh land and was owned by the Island Mill Lumber Company of LaCrosse. A logging camp was located near the dam for several winters giving local farmers employment in winter months.

During the late 1800s, oxen were paired up in teams to haul pine logs up to the creek edges until springtime thaws. Dams were let lose when the time was right, allowing logs to float downstream all the way to Onalaska, Wisconsin, to be sorted for numerous sawmills located there. Logs were marked on the ends with stamp hammers to identify the owners. Logging companies registered their marks, each unique in their own way. Marks consisted of letters and/or symbols. Logs were also chopped with an axe on the side with a unique bark mark, another additional way to identify them. Men called scalers sorted and counted the logs on the Black River, just ahead of the mills, and gave owners credit. Some companies that logged in Sherwood Forest in addition to Island Mill were P. S. Davidson, Waterman & Ketchum, Washburn & Crosby, Atlee, and J. J. Hogan. Most of the companies were based in La Crosse, some in Neillsville.

Tom's Creek, a seasonally navigable stream, starts in the Township of Lynn north of Sherwood. It crosses Highway 73 in two places and then flows east joining the East Fork of the Black River in Section 13. The creek was named for Tom La Flesh, an early settler and lumberman who lived along the creek in Section 3.

Lindsay Creek starts in the northeast part of the township and flows south into Tom's Creek. It is not a navigable stream but it still may have been used for logging purposes back in the late 1800s. One day when crossing the creek I found a horseshoe lying in the creek bed. Lindsay Creek is named for Freeman D. Lindsay, a lumber and businessman from Neillsville, who owned acreage on the upper part of the creek. Freeman never lived in Sherwood but most likely made trips out to oversee his logging operations from time to time. F. D. as he was called, entered the Civil War while living in New York. He later became mayor of Neillsville and Sheriff of Clark County. Freeman is buried in the Neillsville City Cemetery with his wife. He is also the namesake of Lindsey (mistakenly spelled with an "e") in Wood County.

Ladd Creek flows through the south and eastern part of the township into Hay Creek. It was most likely named for the Ladd family who settled early in Sherwood but didn't stay long. William Ladd owned a large farm on the Clark/Jackson County line in Sherwood as early as 1878 and ran a boarding house for those passing through. Herman Ladd owned land near the area where Ladd Creek begins. Now known as Lead Creek, it is not navigable but is great for wildlife habitat.

La Flesh Family Stories

The La Flesh family was off to new adventures by 1887, but the family's early arrival in Sherwood Township, aid in the township's creation, and livelihood in those important early years, can't be overlooked. In 1999, I met Jack La Flesh, grandson of Thomas La Flesh, when he came from California to visit Sherwood, his father's birthplace. Jack was the only descendant to carry on the family name. He was kind enough to share his family history with me and pages he had typed from his Aunt Mary La Flesh Hunter's memoirs of those early days in Sherwood. The writings of Mary give us a wonderful reflection on "the way things were".

Elizabeth Summerside La Flesh, wife of Thomas La Flesh, is thought to have suggested the name for the township as Sherwood Forest in 1876. Elizabeth was a native of England. Elizabeth's father was a minister from England who did mission work in France and Italy. He smuggled bibles under his tall silk hat into the city of Florence. The Summerside family first immigrated to Maine and later settled in Wisconsin where Elizabeth presumably met Thomas. They were married in Black Earth, Wisconsin, during the Civil War.

Thomas La Flesh carried on his logging business and farmed at his "Ranch" in Section 3, for several years along the creek that bears his name. There was a huge log home on the property, many outbuildings, a store to sell supplies to his employees, and a post office at his residence. The post office was named Nevins in honor of La Flesh's good friend from LaCrosse, Sylvester Nevins, who visited often but never lived in Sherwood. Nevins partnered with his brother-in-law, C. C. Washburn, in lumbering and business dealings and was elected to the Wisconsin state senate. Sylvester's origins were from New York and he returned to his home state in his later years.

The Nevins post office continued until the early 1900s, and was later operated by the Byron Pickering family who bought the "Ranch" in about 1888.

Captain Thomas Jefferson La Flesh   (Jack La Flesh Photo)

Tom and Elizabeth had seven children and named their youngest son Thomas Sherwood La Flesh. Their oldest daughter, Mary Serena, or "Mayme", as mentioned earlier, kept journals during her young life. In the 1940s, she referred to them to write her memoir. Unfortunately, she said she destroyed the journals, after finishing her story. Mary gives us an interesting glimpse into early days at Sherwood Forest and excerpts from what her nephew, Jack La Flesh, referred to as her "Chronicle", follow:

"[Referring to her youngest siblings] Thomas Sherwood [La Flesh] was born in Sherwood Forest, Wisconsin, July 28, 1875; Elizabeth Lorena [La Flesh] in Sherwood Forest, August 14, 1878; and Arthur French [La Flesh] in Sherwood Forest, June 13, 1880. The "French" in Arthur's name was for the kind old Doctor [B. F. French] who braved a wild sixteen mile ride [from Neillsville] to come to Mother, when the "June freshets" had swollen all the streams and carried away bridges. Father and Dr. French had to be swum by a man on horseback, riding like a maniac through the night… Aunt Mandy was always so full of nonsense we youngsters loved and I never will forget the perfectly delicious gum she made out of the white pitch we scraped off the ends of the pine logs at the "landing"… We must have gone to Sherwood Forest for the first time when Willie [her brother born in 1869 in Necedah, Wisconsin] was a baby and I was a very little girl. Sherwood Forest was 640 acres in the South East corner of Clark County. Father was lumbering there. At my first remembrance it was a wilderness, a little clearing in a forest. I think every evergreen tree in America grew there, tamarac[k], cedar, fir, spruce, pine and then there were maple trees, oak and one elm. My brother started to chop down the elm tree once and Father bound up the gash and babied the tree, so no harm was done. This was years later, however. I remember the tamarac[k] gum, the hazel nuts, the cranberry marsh and all the wonderfully flavored wild berries, plums and cherries. The house was built of hewn logs and Mother's part was whitewashed on the inside. The other part was a cookhouse for the logging crew and they slept upstairs. It is of these stair steps I have a keen memory. I can see Pat Vaughn, the cook coming after me with a long handled spoon in his hand, he had been stirring something on the stove and I probably thought while his back was turned was my chance to investigate the forbidden territory. I can see myself scrambling up those rude steps and watching Pat out of the corner of my eye. I never did get up those steps – maybe that is why I remember it so clearly. Pat Vaughn, like so many of my father's employees, was with us for many years, - he could bake the finest beans I ever tasted. Cooked in a Dutch oven in a bean hole, made by putting heated rocks in a hole, covering the oven and keeping a slow fire going on top. We children loved Pat Vaughn and "Nigger Bill" who was Father's valet through his officer's days during the war, and Father brought him with him. [Pat Vaughn stayed in Clark County and lived at the Poor Farm in the Town of York and is buried there north of Neillsville. "Nigger Bill" worked for Tom La Flesh the winter of 1885, and in the spring he made the *Neillsville Press* where he was mentioned as entertaining many friends in Neillsville with his "Ole Virginny" eccentricities!] During that first stay in Sherwood Forest, I remember my Mother's story of a grand old dog they had. One day he came to her whining and crying and looking at her with pleasing eyes, trying to tell her something, finally pulling at her dress. Mother followed him and found Jackson, one of the men, who was deaf and dumb. He could make no outcry, and was pinned under the large branch of a fallen tree, in such a manner he was unable to move. Mother had to go for help to extricate the poor man. We always loved that story… We moved back to Sherwood Forest [from north of Neillsville near Cawley Creek] in the spring of 1875 and lived there, sixteen miles from Neillsville, for several years… the happiest days of my life were lived there. It wasn't a wilderness any more. There were acres under cultivation, a small orchard where I have seen the deer jump over the fence to eat the fallen apples. There were barns, cattle, horses, pigs, chickens, everything one could ask for. The "tote team" went to Neillsville for such things as were needed that the farm did not produce… One night I remember hearing a most awful squealing from the hogs, and men rushing around, a couple of gun shots and the next morning a big bear skin was nailed on the blacksmith shop door. The house was enlarged – we had a large living room with Mother's organ at one end and later, when I was eighteen, my piano at the other end, easy chairs, a sofa, reading table, in the winter a big round heater in the center of the room. And the pictures, steel engraving of "Taming the Shrew", a lovely lady in a riding habit who had apparently tamed an unruly horse, "Horse in a Thunder Storm", a chromo of a hunting scene, two dogs waiting under a tree, with the masters coat and gun, another chromo of some prairie chickens, a large wreath of flowers made of vegetable seed and framed in a square box like arrangement with glass. Mother made it and we thought it was beautiful. And my Father's books. Down low on the shelves were Shakespeare and Les Miserable… We had Mother's room opening off the living room and it had an outside door leading into the garden… Upstairs, four bedrooms and a large room over Mother's room where we had many things stored, among them an old gun, we called a "sixteen shooter". One day Willie was sent up to this room for punishment and apparently was amusing himself snapping the trigger on this gun. There was supposed to be a load in the gun which no one had ever been able to dislodge. Mother and Clara Smith, who taught our school that year, were sitting near the stove in Mother's room. Suddenly there was a terrific explosion and a bullet dropped through a beam in the ceiling and fell at Clara's feet. My Mother ran to the stairway door and stood with her hands over her face – not a sound from upstairs. Clara said "let me go". Mother shook her head, opened the door and went up the narrow stairway and there sat Willie on a trunk, the gun lying on the floor. Willie was as black as he could be from the powder, perfectly unharmed, but paralyzed with terror… We were all growing up and Father had built a school house [the original Audubon log school house that later burned down]… These years and many to follow, were years of such plenty that I have never known the worth of money. We had much more than we needed and put no value on anything. If we wanted something, we had it. But our wants were simple then. There were twenty seven cows milked morning and night. Down in the spring house, great pans of milk and jars of butter, certain pans we youngsters could have, cream and all, some the men could drink. I can remember skimming the thick, yellow cream to put over a dish of wild berries. The cold, cold spring in the corner from which we carried our drinking water. We had an ice house where the men stored away chunks of ice cut from Tom's Creek below the house. In the summer we could have ice cream. All our bacon and ham was cured on the farm, pork salted down, and beef corned. Down in the root houses were barrels and barrels of apples, kegs of sour kraut, pickles, mincemeat, everything. Grandmother made vinegar and soft soap. In the spring the maple trees in the grove were tapped and Grandmother superintended the making of maple syrup and sugar. Those were the days, how we loved it – the great black kettles with the bubbling syrup. We would scoop up some snow in a saucer and Grandmother would pour a spoon full of syrup on the snow – it hardened and was simply delicious. Father was a royal host and we entertained many and often. One hunting party consisted of the editor of the New York Sun, Lord Booth and valet [from] England, Mr. Graham from Scotland, Mr. Law and Mr. Hogan of La Crosse, Buffalo Bill (William Cody), White Beaver and another newspaper man from the south, I have forgotten his name. Buffalo Bill and Alice [Mary's sister] became warm friends. Often ex- Governor Washburn and General Crosby visited us. At one time when they came, Mother had a wonderful dinner, with fried chicken as the meat and were we children and probably Mother too, amazed when Governor Washburn asked if he could have a piece of salt pork, fried. We all learned to ride horseback on old Nelly Gray who was spending her last days in the pasture. When Nelly Gray was tired of us, she just stood still and shook us off; always it wasn't near a rock pile… Four of us were going to school now, with six of the McGinnis twelve… and Edith, Helen, and Myron Pickering, and quaint little Emily Sparks, we had quite a school. The McGinnis children walked two miles to school and the Pickering's a mile and a half… On March 14th, 1885, my brother

Willie died from brain concussion, caused by a fall. At Christmas time, Father had given Alice and me each a gold bracelet, - Alice lost hers on the school ground, and as a gang of us were returning from a visit to one of Father's camps, someone told us Cy Stockwell, the new book keeper's son, had found the lost bracelet, so as we drove by the Stockwell home, Willie jumped out of the sleigh and ran towards the house to pick up the bracelet. A clothes line caught him and threw him with considerable force. The ground was frozen and where cattle had stepped when it was soft, there were great hunks of earth as hard as rocks, Willie struck on the back of his head. We helped him home and no one guessed the seriousness of his injury until very shortly before he died. This taking of a fine young life was a terrible blow... Governor Washburn passed away at the Arkansas Hot Springs in 1882... On my 18th birthday Father gave me the Washburn piano, purchased from the estate... Now, in looking back, I think there was trickery after Governor Washburn died, and of course it was a bad time for the lumber interests. Anyway, Father crashed financially and almost mentally for a time. He was home for a while and then he went to California."

The La Flesh family left Sherwood Forest in 1887 and moved into a beautiful newly built home just east of Neillsville. They didn't remain in their new Neillsville home for long. Soon Elizabeth and the children moved on to join Tom in California. There Tom pursued his interests in logging, and also in gold mining, which never panned out. He should have stayed in Sherwood Forest. but when pine logging was done, his finances were failing, and C. C. Washburn was no longer there to back him financially, Tom decided to move on. Today the only things that remain in Sherwood to carry on his memory are the creek named after him and remnants of a logging dam on Tom's Creek. Tom oversaw the construction of this dam, in Section 14, in 1880.

Buffalo Bill's Visit

It's fun to imagine how Buffalo Bill came to Sherwood Forest with his hunting entourage! The big draw for Buffalo Bill was deer hunting, much like it still is today in many ways.

My most accurate guess as to the identities of the people in this photo that I believe was taken in Neillsville in January, 1886, on the group's return from their Sherwood Forest visit are as follows: Back Row L to R: ? ; ? ; Thomas La Flesh; Sylvester Nevins; ? ; ? . Front Row L to R: Buffalo Bill (Col. William Cody); White Beaver (Dr. Frank Powell) of La Crosse; Sir Evelyn Booth of England). The four men in question were most likely C. Smith, New Orleans; David Law, La Crosse; Josephus Emery, La Crosse; and Yank Adams, Chicago.   (Jack La Flesh Photo)

Accompanying Buffalo Bill on his visit to Sherwood in 1886 was his longtime friend, Dr. Frank Powell, nicknamed "White Beaver".

Powell served four terms as mayor of the city of La Crosse. He also sold patent medicine and his best seller was "White Beaver's Cough Cream". Below are a few articles from the local press detailing the excitement in the community generated by this group's visit.

From *Republican & Press* of Neillsville, Wisconsin – Jan. 21, 1886

"Quite a sensation was created in this city last Thursday afternoon by the arrival of "White Beaver," - Dr. Frank Powell, "Buffalo Bill," - Col. Wm. Cody, and their party, who had been spending a few days at the camps of Capt. La Flesh – Nehawga - in Sherwood Forest. Mr. Adams, the editor and publisher of the Chicago Sporting Journal, and champion Finger Billiardist of the World, was one of the party, likewise J. Emory and David Law, of La Crosse. The boys lined the sidewalks in order to get a good view of Buffalo Bill, and it was amusing to hear the youngsters call out to each other, "Here he is!" "Here he is!" Col. Cody is a splendid specimen of manhood, over six feet tall, and as straight as an arrow. He will weigh about 200 pounds. He is in every respect a polished gentleman far different from the generally received idea in regard to him. White Beaver, the present mayor of LaCrosse, and whose name is often mentioned as a strong candidate for the office of Governor of Wisconsin next fall, is also a fine looking specimen of humanity, and has the reputation of being one of the best physicians and surgeons of the State. The party left Friday evening for La Crosse, having heartily enjoyed their trip to the Clark County woods and Neillsville."

A "thank you" was printed in the local press after the group's visit, listing people from both Clark and Wood County who had entertained them. Those mentioned were; Dick Fahey, Tom and Elizabeth La Flesh, Mrs. Reddan, F. D. Lindsay, E. H. Markey, and Mike Post who worked for Tom La Flesh.

From the *Evening Star* of La Crosse, Wisconsin
CRACK SHOTS IN THE WILDERNESS

"The party which left here a few days ago for a visit to the pine woods of Wisconsin returned to La Crosse this morning. Every member of the party expressed himself delighted with the trip and everything connected with it. Col. Cody says speaking of the pine district, "There the latch string hangs out on the edge of the timber, and not on the doors. Cow-boy hospitality I thought was at the top notch, but that of the timber of Wisconsin, is as great. It is said that Yank Adams sang a thousand songs and out told a million stories, but the shooting was limited. Yank Adams killed three bears, for Yank told us so himself. A number of logging camps were visited, and everywhere the people turned out to welcome the guests, and to make their visit one of the pleasantest ever enjoyed. About ten o'clock this forenoon a large party gathered in White Beaver's shooting gallery to witness a match between Dr. D. F. Powell and Johnny Baker, "The Cow Boy Kid," against Col. Cody and Mr. E. Booth, the champion wing shot of England. Ten shots apiece was the limit, "White Beaver" and "The Kid" winning with a score of 239 out of a possible 240. Buffalo Bill and E. Booth followed close with a score of 238 out of a possible 240. This was a remarkable match, for it was shot by four of the greatest marksmen of the world. And the result of the match shows their wonderful skill with the rifle.

White Beaver and Buffalo Bill have long been acknowledged the most skillful rifle men in the world and "The Kid' is the champion boy shot of the world, Mr. Booth's weapon is the shotgun but his work with the rifle is very fine. The following named gentlemen witnessed the match, and all pronounced it the best exhibition of rifle shooting ever witnessed by them: M. J. Emery, Mr. David Law, and Mr. O. Z. Martin, of Titusville, Penn., Cole Burke, James Bladen, Mac Donaldson, Chas. H. Smith, Yank Adams, and Fred. W. Burke. The visitors returned to the east this evening, each one carrying with him pleasant recollections of his visit to the pine woods of Wisconsin. They leave behind them friends who wish them a safe journey with hopes of another meeting in the near future."

THE POWELL-CODY HUNTING PARTY RETURNS FROM THE WOODS
From the *Republican and Leader* of La Crosse, WI, Jan. 16, 1886

"The famous party of sportsmen, which left this place last Monday, returned last night, much pleased with the trip. A number of deer and smaller game were brought down, but the sport was a little tame for these men some of whom have been wont to drive the buffalo to his death, beard the grizzly in his den and court the face of the fierce red-skin. But the time was pleasantly spent, nevertheless, aided by the unbounded hospitality of the people with whom they met. Buffalo Bill, in speaking of this today, said: "I have always thought cowboy hospitality as being on the top notch, but the hospitality we met with in the woods beats it; the latch string was hung at the edge of the woods…"

Boom Times – 1880s

The 1880s found plenty of activity in Sherwood Forest. From the press we learned that Hugh Perkins was setting up his sawmill operation in 1883, in Section 26, near where he lived with his wife, Matilda, and their children. He partnered with David Geary and purchased a 35 horse power steam sawmill from Milwaukee, arranging for its shipment by train to City Point that fall. The mill had the potential of cutting 20,000 board feet of lumber per day. Hugh also built a large boarding house near the mill area.

Thomas La Flesh started up a shingle saw mill at his farm in December of 1882, and was making three grades of pine shingles each marked with his name, "T. J. La Flesh, Nevins, Wisc.". In 1883 he had 300,000 shingles piled up by his mill in Section 3.

Benjamin Seeley had a steam saw mill set up at his farm on Section 20, one that was somewhat portable.

The Island Mill Lumber Company made improvements of Hay Creek by booming up its banks and straightening out some of the curves. Hay Creek previously was nothing but a little stream flowing through the alders. J. S. Bailey of Black River Falls was overseeing the work and was employed as head foreman for Island Mill in 1881. And the "turnpike" as the press called it, was being greatly improved between Sherwood Forest and City Point.

Deer were plentiful, according to the press, but only one Sherwood man, unnamed, had the time to hunt them. He shot thirteen deer in the winter of 1882. And Ben Seeley, from the south half of town, shot a bear.

Hugh Perkins made a bad move in 1884 at his Sherwood Forest sawmill. His unfortunate story and that of his brother, Miner, follows.

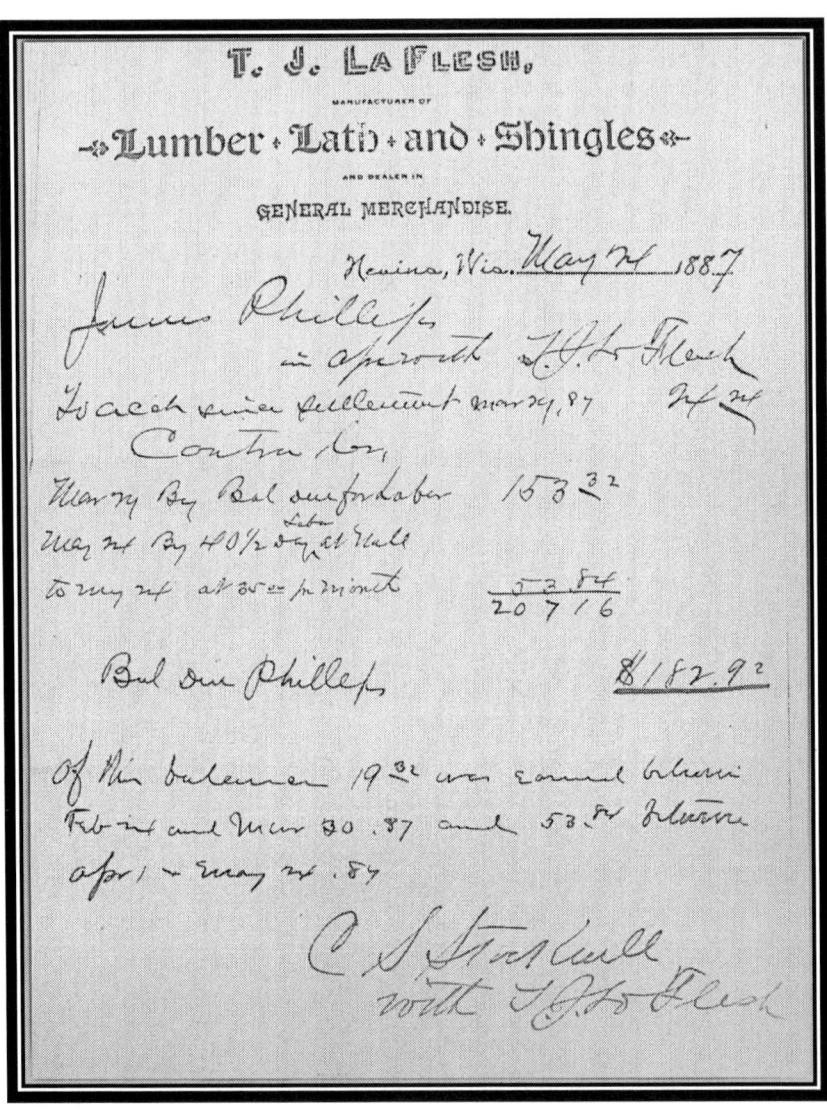

Receipt from T. J. La Flesh of Nevins, Wis. dated May of 1887

Perkins Family Stories

It's uncertain what brought the Perkins family to Sherwood, but for years they were the subject of conversation because of their poor choices. Daniel Chapman Perkins lived near the logging dam at Hay Meadow Creek, the little creek that now feeds Sherwood Lake. Mr. Perkins brought several family members with him from Waushara County, Wisconsin, in the early 1870s. Two grown sons, Miner and Hugh, were both active in the community. Miner first purchased land near Sherwood Bluff and later cooked for a logging camp in the Town of Cary next door. Hugh Perkins farmed, purchased his own steam sawmill and sawed lumber for neighbors. Both brothers found themselves in a heap of trouble, stirring up emotions in the community for years to come.

On a Saturday morning, May 31, 1884, a tragic incident occurred in Sherwood Forest at Hugh Perkin's mill in Section 26. It was a day that would be talked about far and wide for decades; something that should have never happened. A neighbor, Isaac Meddaugh, had brought logs to the mill to be sawed earlier in the week and came back with his brother Robert to load up his lumber and haul it home that morning. When Isaac asked Hugh to measure the load so he knew what to pay him, they started arguing. The heated discussion ended when Hugh pulled out his revolver and shot Isaac in the chest. Isaac fell to the ground and died on the mill floor within just a few minutes. Robert Meddaugh luckily dodged a few more of Hugh's bullets.

Hugh and Isaac had fought the evening before at the mill when Isaac grabbed him by the shirt collar and, to put it bluntly, asked Hugh to quit fooling around with his younger sister, Kitty. Several neighbors witnessed the tussle that Friday night, perhaps even Hugh's wife.

Shortly after the shooting, Hugh rode his horse up the road a few miles and gave himself up to Town Constable, C. S. Stockwell (the book keeper that lived next door to Tom La Flesh and kept track of his logging affairs). Stockwell brought Hugh to the Clark County Sheriff at Neillsville where Perkins was locked up in the county jail and charged with murder. Perkins claimed self-defense and was to be held in jail until the next circuit court date the following December. Several months later, in November of 1884 on Election Day in Neillsville, the town was bustling with excitement. Three prisoners took advantage of the distraction and broke free from the jail after clubbing the turnkey. Hugh Perkins was among the escapees, the others were men named Martin and George Morrison. Martin was being held for murder also, while Morrison was jailed for horse theft. Here is the description given for the escaped Perkins in the local newspaper –"About 40 years old, about 5 feet and 8 inches tall, light complexion, black hair and blue eyes."

Hugh was on the run for almost four years. In October of 1888, he was arrested at Windsor, Ontario, Canada, and returned to the Clark County Jail in Neillsville by Sheriff Dwyer. Hugh gave away his identity when he tried to apply for a Civil War pension in Detroit, Michigan, earlier that year. The pension application gave his whereabouts and led detectives on his trail.

On January 30, 1889, Hugh, while awaiting trial, was released under a bail of $6,000. with financial backing from a few Neillsville businessmen. Shortly before the trial finally occurred in June of 1889, both a captain and a lieutenant of Hugh's old civil war company were interviewed at Neillsville about the case. Perkins was found guilty of manslaughter in the first degree but within one week he was granted a new trial. One of the jurors, prior to the trial, was said to have expressed the opinion that Hugh was guilty and that he'd like to see him sentenced. This technicality allowed Hugh to stay out on bail until a second trial came up at the next regular term of circuit court in December of 1889.

Mention was made in a local newspaper that in September of 1889 Hugh Perkins killed a black bear and brought it to town. The press article said it was a small bear weighing a little over 100 pounds.

In December when Circuit Court came into session, Hugh was retried and the original charge of manslaughter in the first degree was reduced to manslaughter in the second degree. A motion for a new trial was overruled, but a leave was granted to renew the motion at any time.

Hugh was sentenced to five years in the state prison at Waupun, Wisconsin, where he was taken and locked up for about one year. During this year the case was taken to the Supreme Court on appeal and the conviction was reversed with a third trial ordered on grounds of error in the ruling of the court on the admission of certain testimony. Hugh was released on bail from the state prison and on June 12, 1891, he became a free man. The judge recommended a *nolle prosequi*. The prosecution was discontinued because it was felt that the law as interpreted by the Supreme Court would not uphold a conviction. The Neillsville Republican Press editor at the time felt that Mr. Perkins year of imprisonment, agony while awaiting trials, and fear of being caught during his four years as a fugitive were probably sufficient punishment to fit the crime committed. The entire expense to Clark County during the duration of Hugh's case was estimated to be greater than $3,500.

Hugh Perkins never returned to Sherwood Forest after his prison time. He moved to Hay Springs, Nebraska, with his wife, Matilda, (she had found her way to him in Canada while he was hiding out there). Hugh lived in Hay Springs until his wife passed away there many years later. He met his next wife in Hot Springs, Arkansas, while on a retreat there to remedy his ailments. Josephine, a young nurse, married Hugh and the two of them moved to St. Cloud, Florida, in 1924. Hugh died in 1930, at the age of 86, at St. Cloud and was buried there.

Hugh Perkins proudly fought with Company I, 7th Wisconsin Infantry during the Civil War, known as the Iron Brigade, and spent time as a prisoner at Belle Island. Perhaps he suffered from PTSD from years in the war and being held as a prisoner of war. Hugh was active with St. Cloud's G.A.R. post for several years and never shared much of his past with his Florida friends.

While I'm writing about Perkins troubles I might as well share the added troubles of Miner Perkins, Hugh's younger brother. In the fall of 1887, Miner worked for one of the J. W. Knapp logging camps as a camp cook. This particular camp was located about five miles east of Sherwood Forest near the Rocky Run Creek.

On December 19th, 1887, Miner shot and killed his wife, Lottie, with his 34 caliber revolver. The incident occurred during a jealous rage at their residence in the logging camp where the couple lived and worked. Perkins found a letter his wife had written to a male friend just before the shooting. Miner told the logging crew he worked with that his wife had committed suicide. He was arrested, and later confessed to the murder when it became clear to everyone that the angle the bullet struck his wife made it impossible for her to have shot herself.

Miner was sentenced to a life term in the state prison at Waupun. His wife, Lottie (Lamb) Perkins, was buried in Woodlawn Cemetery in Pittsville.

Miner Perkins was released from the state prison, on parole, thirty-two years later. He would have been about 64 years old when he gained his freedom. The greatest victim of this Perkins tragedy was Miner and Lottie's 9 year old son, Guy, their only living child, who was raised by his mother's relatives.

Daniel Perkins, the patriarch, was a Civil War veteran also. One day Daniel set out on foot from his home near what is now Sherwood Park. He headed off to City Point to catch a train intending to ride to Milwaukee for a G.A.R. (Grand Army of the Republic) Civil War Reunion, one he tried to attend annually. Walking from Sherwood to City Point was not uncommon for these early settlers. Daniel carried a satchel with him that day and when a heavy rain caused Hay Meadow Creek to rise higher than he cared to cross, he laid down to rest in the woods near the swollen creek. Several days later, Daniel was found lying there as if sleeping, with his satchel under his head as his pillow, dead to the world. After an inquest of the body was made, and no foul play suspected, Daniel was buried near his last resting place, in the woods by Hay Meadow Creek.

Myron Pickering & The Bear Trapper

During the 1880s another City Point resident moved north to Sherwood Forest onto a landlocked, wooded forty acres, hoping for privacy and a chance to continue his unique vocation as a bear trapper. His name was Franklin Edwin Dartt, a subject of curiosity for many people, even many years beyond his death, in 1918. Frank moved from Vermont to Wisconsin when a young boy, with his parents who farmed in Marquette County. He came to City Point Township, near Spaulding in the 1880s and purchased a 40 acre landlocked parcel a half mile from the nearest town road, in Section 25, at Sherwood Forest, in 1893. A noisy sawmill next door to his City Point location was said to be the reason for his move about ten miles north to Sherwood.

"Eccentric" and "hermit" were two words frequently used to describe Frank Dartt. He was a bachelor and lived in a small log home with a large enclosed pit nearby to house the bears he trapped. The bears were often kept alive until their fur was prime. Dartt then sold the live bears, bear meat, and bear hides. He had an extensive trap line and owned at least 50 large leg hold bear traps.

An interesting story about Frank Dartt can best be told from the memoir of Myron Pickering, a young man who was hired to help Dartt run a trap line in the late 1800s. This memoir was generously shared with me by Myron's granddaughter, Dorothy Pickering Bullington, of Montana. As mentioned earlier, the Byron Pickering family moved to Sherwood Forest in the 1870s and lived along Tom's Creek in Section 10. They later purchased the La Flesh Ranch and ran the post office called Nevins until the early 1900s when they moved out west. Here are Myron's words from his memoir written in about 1964, when he was 91 years old and living in Montana.

"I suppose there are more memories grouped in the month of September 1889 than any other month of my life.

At that time we had just finished building a ten-room house and were moved in and as my folks had the post office [Nevins], people from the whole neighborhood came to our home for their mail. Among them was Frank Dartt, the bear trapper.

On the first of September, 1889, Mr. Dartt came for his mail and asked if I would work for him through September. To me this was like a great adventure and I took him up on the deal and got ready to go, and as I loved hunting, was taking my gun along. But Mr. Dartt said I would not need it, which spoiled some of my hopes of a good time. But still there would be the adventure of catching bears.

When I came to experience a trapper's life, I found it was not all play, for we had a trail six miles in one direction from camp and three in the other that had to be patrolled every day, looking after 45 traps. Mr. Dartt went with me over the line and then made it my job to patrol the six mile line, and he the three mile. In the month I was with him I think we caught 13 bears, so you see we had a bear to take care of about every two or three days.

Of course the first bear caught gave me by far the greatest excitement, for it was so new and wonderful to think of handling, caging, and hauling home a real wild bear.

I quickly found that it was not only a very important experience for me, but for Mr. Dartt also for before dropping the cage over the bear he had to take many precautions. One of these was to tie the 15' long trap clog to a tree tying the trap with the bear up so to speak. He then set the bear cage with open bottom toward the bear, so that when close enough the cage would drop over the bear. A board for the bottom could be pushed in; then the foot with the trap had to be taken care of. It was here I got one of my most important lessons, for before starting to cage the bear Mr. Dartt gave me the clamps for removing the trap when the bear was in the cage.

Well, he yelled to me, "Give me the clamps!" In all the excitement I had laid the clamps down somewhere and I had forgotten where, and what was I to do? I'm sure my heart cried out, "God, help me!" I don't think it took a minute to find them, but it seemed like an hour.

The fact that Mr. Dartt had given me the responsibility of those clamps and that for the moment was my only job, and I so utterly failed, was driven home so the lesson had a permanent effect on my life."

THE FOREST FIRE "I don't remember how we learned of it, but we somehow knew a forest fire was moving in our direction and it meant fast and energetic action if we were to save our traps and building from destruction. A forest fire of this kind without wind to drive it creeps rather slowly, giving time to prepare for its arrival, such as picking up things that fire would damage and laying out lines of defense for stopping it when it arrives.

The job given me was to go over the trap line and take up all the traps and hang them up on trees which I did. Starting in the evening I went the six miles and took up the traps, but when it came my usual bedtime I became so sleepy I laid down on the ground and slept, actually only a few minutes, but that was the total sleep for me for that night and also the night following, for we laid out a large piece of ground on which the buildings were located. By utilizing trails, roads, and a stream surrounding the same, and constantly patrolling day and night for two nights and two days we saved the home ground and all the buildings. It did not take the fire that long to pass by, but there were many fires that lingered after, in stumps and dead trees from which the wind sometimes blew sparks quite a distance and started new fires which had to be attended quickly to prevent them from getting out of control. Hence, after the main fire had passed, there was a watch job for a time.

As time went on, caging and hauling in bears became routine and the log enclosure became quite crowded. We fed the bears in shallow feeding containers like cupboard drawers that we could pull out to put in the corn which was the diet, about the same as hogs. But the bears showed better intelligence for each had his own trough and he would wait until he heard the feed poured into his trough, which was pulled out to fill. He would take hold of his end with the claws of his front paw and pull it in with a bang.

When I finished my month, Mr. Dartt figured two extra days for the firefighting and I would not take it, for I wanted to share his misfortune; and so to show his appreciation, at Christmas time when he butchered his bears for the Chicago market, he brought us a nice shoulder of bear meat."

The *Neillsville Press* mentioned what could have been this memorable fire in May of 1887. The fire, according to two businessmen who rode out to Nevins, was to have started near the town line between Washburn and Levis and burned all the way eastward through the timber half way across Sherwood Forest. Luckily it missed homesteads, but killed millions of feet of good pine. The pine would have to be harvested the following winter or be lost according to the press. Two logging camps on the East Fork were said to have burned, including all sleds and camp equipment.

When Byron and Hannah Sparks Pickering took over the La Flesh ranch and Nevins post office they were quite active in the community. Byron served on the town board and held church services in his home. He hired several neighbors to work for him sawing wood and bought extra flour and supplies from town to share with others. Byron won the low bid to build the new Audubon School house on property he deeded to the school, in 1891, after the log school burned down on the neighboring Scholtz property. Pickering also bid on and built the town hall in 1891 for $500. on half an acre of land sold to the township for $20. by Stillman Ellis. The hall was used for church services for many years after it was first built, also for funerals, as well as town meetings. In the 1890s revival meetings were held there and many "came to the altar" and dedicated their lives to God in this same town hall that is still in use today in Sherwood.

Old man Dartt, as many of the locals called Frank, continued to trap bear in Sherwood for many years and remains of several large hand dug pits where he kept his bears can still be seen today. Originally the pits were seven to eight feet deep but are filling in with time. Perhaps the largest pit yet visible was the one with the log enclosure over the top of it. When Frank was ready to sell his bears he would load them in his iron cage mounted on top of a wagon, hitch up his horses to the wagon, and haul them to the nearest railroad depot. Alice (Ferguson) Qualley, late resident of Washburn Township, Clark County, recalled that the sled he pulled behind his horse looked like an airplane. Perhaps it had extensions on the sides so the live bears inside wouldn't tip the wagon over.

A couple recollections from the Hughes brothers who lived at Kurth Corners, central Grant Township, Clark County, on what is now State Hwy 10, were that Dartt used honey as bait to attract the bears into his traps. They also remembered seeing him pass by in late fall on his way to Neillsville with a load of bear meat and bear pelts.

One kind of trap that Dartt used was a #5 Newhouse double long-spring leghold. This trap had a jaw spread of nearly 12 inches, weighed 17 pounds, and required special tools for most people to set it. A 1902 Sears Roebuck catalog sold this trap for $5.00. along with the setting clamps that Myron Pickering spoke of.

Dartt sometimes had trouble with people stealing his traps and his furs. He was a bit suspicious of loggers who worked near his property and worried about them cutting down his pine trees on the outer edges of his parcel. In those days it was common for loggers to encroach onto others property, especially if there was no one living there.

In January of 1898, Frank bought another 40 acre parcel that connected to his on the west side from the Island Mill Lumber Company. He paid $40.00 for this parcel with the stipulation that Island Mill reserve the right to enter the land and harvest all the pine timber if and when they wanted to.

The number of bears in Sherwood Forest began to dwindle in the latter 1890s. About this time Frank Dartt dabbled in bee keeping. Perhaps the meat market at Chicago was changing as well so he began collecting bee hives and continued with this for many years. Dartt even taught the neighbor kids how to go about the whole process and young Paul Schwanebeck was one who took an interest. Paul kept up with bee keeping himself and it became a lifelong hobby for him. Many of the neighbors would head over to Dartt's to purchase their honey.

Dartt didn't take any slack to law violators. One day he and Hans C. Anderson, a bachelor who lived near Sherwood Bluff, followed some hunters who had shot a couple of deer and watched where they hid them. Either Dartt or Anderson walked all the way to City Point, 8 miles, to alert the game warden, George K. Redmond, who confiscated the deer.

Frank apparently didn't like wolves and put poison out for them in 1909. Sometimes the neighbors' dogs got into it and died. One who lost a dog this way was Clarence Freedlund in the winter of 1910.

Sherwood folks thought Dartt had a lot of money and might have hoarded it somewhere on his property. As Frank grew older he would hire locals to do chores for him but would always ask them to return the following day for their pay. This made people wonder if Dartt kept his money buried somewhere near his home.

In May of 1918 Frank Dartt passed away at the age of about 76 at his Sherwood home, records make it difficult to tell how old he actually was but he was not nearly as old as some made him out to be. He'd been ill for a short time and some of the locals were making sure he had food to eat and tried to help take care of him. His shack was pretty much in shambles when he died. After his passing, Town Chairman, John Coulthard, searched his place to locate any money that might be lying around and turn it over to the county appointed administrator of the estate. Coulthard worked at getting Frank's personal property ready to sell so his estate could be settled and fed Frank's horse for a month. Dartt's fifty bear traps were sold to Albert Gall in a bunch for $12.00. His black bear skin overcoat was sold for $5.00. Two iron bear cages were sold to a man in Colby for $6.00. Frank's estate also included 275 beehives, extracting machinery, platform scales, three guns, two caldron kettles, and a silver watch.

Dartt's nephew, Royal Dartt, from Montello, Wisconsin, took his remains back home for burial in a Dartt family lot there but never purchased a gravestone. Royal was miffed, thought Frank had more money than he did and also thought there was a will that should have left it all to him. No will was found, just $400. in drafts by Chairman John Coulthard.

After Frank's passing, locals remembered seeing the ground surrounding his cabin all dug up. I'll quote from a letter written to me from Helen Seman (age 93) in 1997. The Seman's lived on the La Flesh/Pickering farm for many years - *"It seems to me like we bought a gallon of honey from Frank Dart, never heard what he did for a living or much about him. This happened long ago - my brother, Joe, was on the town board at one time and when that party living on the road west of the town hall died, Joe went over to the place to look things over and he said the ground was all spaded up. Someone thought maybe he buried some money or something there."* If a stash was found, no one told. Myron Pickering thought the same thing.

Myron, then living in Montana, sent a letter to the editor when he heard about Frank Dartt's death and it was published in the *Neillsville*

Republican & Press, June 20, 1918. "... I was escorted to his lodge by a neighbor, who had learned the way to his headquarters. They were located at the head of a small meadow creek with pine and hardwood growing so thickly on either side that they nearly shaded the little opening where the buildings were located. I well remember the peculiar sensations that the many sounds of animals, birds and falling acorns gave me when rising at daybreak on those September mornings to take care of the horses and bears and get ready for an early start on five miles of traps I usually watched...On one occasion I discovered a trap with the twenty-five foot sapling used for a log gone. The trail led straight into a dense thicket of saplings, blackberry briars and windfall timber, thru which I followed it at least a half a mile, expecting all the time to hear the rattle of the chain or other noise that usually accompanies such a circumstance; but nothing of the kind happened for as I opened an especially thick bunch of brush imagine my surprise to find myself facing a four hundred pound bruin almost within striking distance of my face... Evidently he was as scared as I for he allowed me to quietly back away out of reach and I hastened to report to Mr. Dartt. An hour later he, with some long, sharp stakes crept close enough to the bear to stake the ring of the chain to the ground, after which we proceeded to the caging process.. Another time...after working until evening we had started for camp when I, hearing a sound much like a cow bellowing, and remarked to Mr. Dartt on the strange circumstance of a cow so far from civilization. Stopping to listen he informed me it was not a cow but a bear experiencing the first pangs of the jaws of the seventeen pound trap...Coming up to the perpetrator of the unearthly bellows in the person was a cub bear about six or eight months old; and although I was never permitted to carry my rifle with me, on this occasion Mr. Dartt had his and gave it to me to hold off the old she bear who threatened us from the brush nearby while he caged the cub...This was not the only occasion when I heard the voice of the bear for when a new recruit was added to the bear pen there was always a night of the fiercest howling and wailing... The last day of my stay with Mr. Dartt it happened that one of his bear died and he asked my assistance investigating the circumstances. The place where the bears were kept was a large log enclosure with log covering and a partition of logs making two parts with a slide door between, and the dead bear was in the back compartment which had no exit from the outside. After an assurance that all the live bears were in the other part and the door closed, by his request I held a lamp in thru a feed hole that he might look down thru a crack from above to see the dead bear. While holding the lamp I felt something cold touch my arm and not knowing what it was, peeked into the opening only to discover the brown nose of a bear on my arm. To say the lamp was removed abruptly is saying it easy. Mr. Dartt had overlooked one bear, and she was not the kind that gets scared at a light either... They naturally display their pugilistic tendencies by striking viscously at anyone who ventured too near the cage or peep holes in the pen. Before I learned this I got a shirt sleeve torn and four deep claw marks on my arm....I often wondered that no one was seriously injured at the peep hole in the pen where visitors often looked at them. Mr. Dartt was honest to the cent. I had reasons to believe his money was buried in the woods near his home. Taking everything into consideration, I can remember no month of my life more profitably spent than the one with the trapper and hunter, Frank Dartt."

Many years after his death, Dartt's lifestyle remained a topic of local conversation and some still ponder about Frank Dartt to this day and the mystery of his wealth. The Sherwood Bluff was referred to by some locals in the 1930s as Dartt Hill. It is located just one half mile south of the Dartt homestead. A logging dam and a creek, west and southwest of Dartt's land, were called Dartt Dam and Dartt Creek for a time by Sherwood locals.

Myron's Memoirs

Referring back to Myron Pickering's memoirs, whose writings gave us such a wonderful insight into the life of Frank Dartt, I want to share his reflections about early days in Sherwood Forest. Myron began his memoir by saying how thankful to God he was for his heritage and the experiences he had as a young lad growing up in Sherwood Forest before "the age of modern inventions". His words about lumbering, hunting, the pine forest, and firefighting give us such a unique glimpse into Sherwood's history and that is the reason I have dedicated so much text to Myron Pickering.

"I was born in Nevins, Wisconsin [in 1873] when the logging was being cleared off there. My father and others were making most of their living by working in logging camps. That was in the day when the primitive methods were changing into the more modern. I was about five years old when they were beginning to saw down trees instead of chopping them down. I can remember my dad saying, "Those Norwegians are sawing down trees instead of chopping them." Before that it was the custom to have an expert chopper. Then two men with a saw would go along and saw them into logs. Before sawing them into logs they sawed off the end where the ax had left an uneven shape. With the new method of sawing the trees, it revolutionized that part of the west.

I lived in a day when the settlers didn't know anything about a mowing machine. People raised stock but the feed had to be cut from the marshes with a scythe, or what they called the "Armstrong method." Men would mow with a scythe, bring it together with a hand rake, and pull it in with a pair of oxen on a pung. They didn't even have wagons at that time. In that hard way they would get feed for their stock. They would visit from home to home, taking their family in what they called "pungs." It was just a sort of sled that was pulled over the ground by a yoke of oxen. It was very slow... a man would cut the grain and two men would come along and tie it in bundles by hand.

At that time the lumber industry was moving across that section of the country. They moved the logs down by water. There was a small stream [Tom's Creek] right across my father's place and below our place about a half mile they built a dam. It was just high enough so they could raise the water in the creek to several feet in depth in the spring. Above this dam they placed the logs. The logs were hauled in by teams of the logging companies. They used sleds and made their roads with iced strips for the runners. They moved very large loads of logs to this place where the dam had made a lake. In the spring when the water was running they closed the dam until the pond was full and the logs were floating. Then when they opened the gates it was a wonderful sight to see the logs come rushing through the sluiceway and go tumbling end over end in the large body of water to the next dam which would be perhaps four or five miles further downstream. By repeating this process they moved a large volume of logs to the mills.

One of my earlier memories was when my dad built his log cabin on the homestead. At that time the neighbors got together and sawed the logs and built the cabin that we lived in. I can well remember how the pine trees were felled and shaped and cut and put into the house…

As time went on and I got older and went to school we had another kind of pleasure – that of associating with other kids at school. We had a swimming hole and at noon time, when it was warm enough we had wonderful times swimming.

I think I was about 13 or 14 years old when I got courageous enough to ask my dad, "Dad, can I take the shotgun?" I don't know how I got the courage to do it. In those days kids were not carrying guns around promiscuously. But I asked Dad, "Can I take the gun and go hunting?" He said "O.K." He got the old ten gauge, double barreled shotgun, set up a target on a stump and said, "Try to hit that." I remember I took two shots. I didn't do very well but I hit the target. And everything was lovely. That day I didn't do much hunting. I just traveled around in the woods. I didn't get anything that time. But it wasn't long before I was able to go out and get the game. That shotgun was the feather of that day. My dad usually used it and he left it to me with the old musket."

Hannah (Sparks) & Byron Pickering
Myron's Parents – (Dorothy Pickering Bullington Photo)
Byron and his sons built the Sherwood town hall in 1891 after winning the low bid in the township of $500. The Pickering family also built the Audubon school house which still stands today.

Myron continued, "By the way, I'll have to tell you about that musket. It was a civil war musket. My dad was a civil war veteran. Whether this was the same gun he used in the war I'm not able to say, but it was the same kind. With it he killed many deer. He told me some experiences with that gun that were interesting. One was when he was traveling home from the neighbors where he'd been helping. On the way home through the woods he saw a buck deer. He shot it. Then he casually loaded his gun and was walking on, when another one came walking along. He killed it. It was a very large buck. Again he was casually loading his gun when another came along and got the same treatment. In those days it was pretty necessary to get the deer meat because they didn't have other kind of meat. They weren't raising enough livestock and the deer came in pretty handy. It was a common thing to have a deer lick and go sit in a runway where the deer were used to going. They would put a string across, with a loaded gun that he would trip as he went across it, and that way catch a deer. The old musket was used even for that…

On another occasion Dad took his musket as he climbed a tree over the deer lick to wait for the deer. It was too dark to see but he could hear two bucks fighting. He shot by guess but couldn't be sure what the result of his shot was and he went home for the night. In the morning he went to look, taking his dog with him. He saw there was blood, so he set the dog on the track into the woods. The dog soon found the deer and waited until Dad came with his gun and some buckshot. He shot at the deer which was facing him and the skull was so hard that the buckshot wouldn't penetrate it. He was making a lunge for Dad when the dog caught him by the hind foot and held him. Dad wasn't sure but the buck would have killed him if the dog hadn't caught him…"

Sherwood Forest Hunters – Circa 1895
Left to Right: David Sparks, David Pickering, Earl Pickering, Myron Pickering.　　　　　　　　　　　(Pickering Family Photo)

"There were few improved roads and where they crossed swampy ground, men made what they called corduroy, by bridging the swampy places with small log ridges which were not so bad for sleighs but for wagons, which fortunately were not many, they were terrible as anyone can imagine.

I lived about half-way between two schools which were about four miles apart [Audubon and Birdland Echo], so it was possible for me to go to either one I chose. It was interesting to see the difference in grades and morals of these schools. Much of the time there was no Sunday school or church but occasionally a traveling missionary would visit and give a Sunday sermon. Maybe he preached the truth and maybe not but many of the people did not know the difference. In case of a wedding or funeral they had to call for some preacher from a distance and it was usually a Freewill Baptist who lived sixty miles away, [Myron's uncle Robert Davenport Sparks of Plainfield] but was related to some of the people of the neighborhood.

The winter and spring were filled with activities in and about the logging operations which had their excitement and tragedies. I remember vividly when I saw my mother weeping and a neighbor asking her what was the trouble, and she said a man had been killed by a falling tree and they were making a coffin and shroud for the body. I remember that when hunting many years later my father showed the very tree that crushed him to the ground. In those days there were no legal problems involved, but in this case the corpse had to be put in a box, taken to the nearest station, and shipped home, 60 miles away. [The man who died was most likely Thomas Bound, a distant relative of the Sparks family, who lived in Waushara County, Wisc.]

Shortly after this the same man who tried to comfort Mother, saying maybe he isn't dead," rode by my home and surrendered himself... The man's name was Hugh Perkins. Ike Meddaugh had demanded that he cease relations with his sister, Kit. Therefore Perkins forbade him to come to the sawmill again, but as Meddaugh was having his lumber sawed in this mill, and came to see about his lumber, Perkins shot him and he was carried home... The neighborhood was very worked up and some thought he should be lynched... he never again did business here...

Events, developments and changes passed quickly as the harvest of the white pine forest moved through that section of the country and right across the creek, a little more than a stone's throw away, was the edge of a quarter section of solid pine with beautiful deep shade in some places. It's doubtful if the direct rays of the sun ever reached the ground.

A logging outfit was built just across the creek [Tom's Creek] which consisted of a large cook and dining shanty, a large sleeping building, and a large barn for the horses. The crew consisted of sawyers who felled and sawed the trees into logs (usually 12', 14', and 16' lengths) and the swampers who trimmed off the limbs and made a clear path to the logs, the skidders who put them on a skidway in shape to load on sleds. From there they were hauled to the landing in the creek above the dam where they waited only until the spring thaw would furnish flood water to float them down the river to the mill, maybe 100 miles away.

As it happens, this was the last of the river log driving in that section of the country. It was interesting to me, a 12 year old, to watch those operations. Sunday was wash day or rest day if they wished. To me, a kid, it was interesting to see one man pull a pistol out of his pocket and bring down a woodcock at quite a distance. In those days we never heard of a man being arrested for carrying a pocket gun and some of the boys became fairly good shots. My brother, later, bagged two deer with a pocket gun.

They finished that forest that winter and after that the small mills began the work of harvesting the smaller forests of hardwood. But transition from one kind of operation to another had a tragic effect on some of the people who had depended on harvesting pine forests for a living."

Myron then explained how his father was able to purchase the La Flesh ranch in the late 1880s, after getting help with financing from a Neillsville businessman. It was the end of the white pine logging era for the most part, and where Mary La Flesh (in her chronicle), mentioned her family moving from Sherwood Forest to Neillsville. This was a sad time for the La Flesh family but also a happy time for the Pickering family. Their lives were filled with new opportunities when they moved from their tiny log shack along Tom's Creek to a working farm just a mile to the north.

Myron was 13 years old when the family moved to the ranch and he continues his memoir to talk about their new home. "… From then on Dad could accumulate sheep and hogs and a little dairy herd. He had horses to run the place with. My mother began to raise a nice large flock of barred Plymouth rocks and things looked pretty good. This became the stopping place for all the preachers that came along. It was a place of hospitality; friends from all kinds of places came to visit. There was a long table in our kitchen that would seat a dozen or more people and it wasn't uncommon to have the table full. That's the kind of hospitality that was shown in my home and I thank God for that kind of home.

The Nevins Sawmill – (Pickering Family Photo)

One of the features of my mother's table was that when the strawberries were on Mother would make real dripping pans full of short – real shortcake. Two layers, covered nicely with butter, and then bring on the berries…

My story of my childhood would be far from complete if I passed over some of the effects of the harvesting of the dense forests. One thing was the enormous amount of residue left behind in the form of tree tops, limbs, and boughs, which covered the ground where the forest had been. When the forest stood in its natural, living form the ground was kept moist by the dense shade so that there was nothing for a fire hazard. But now that the shade was gone, and the ground covered with powder-dry, pitch-filled remains, it was only a matter of time until a great explosion was to occur, which, when it did occur, was something never to be forgotten.

As I write this, I call to mind two occasions when I personally had the experience of not only observing, but fighting such a fire, and as I have said, this condition lay just a short distance across the creek from our home. I don't remember, perhaps I never knew, how or where it started, but I presume it moved toward us from some distance away, for I well remember a neighbor from a mile away being with us in the fight.

We found it necessary to backfire, which we did by going across the creek and starting a fire that we could control, letting it go to meet the incoming inferno. As we did this we found our backfire became a giant. It was all we were able to handle and I can never forget how we fought with water from the creek, and whipped it with wet bags. But such a hot fire rather quickly burns itself out. When it was over we were a pretty mussed up looking bunch. A very interesting feature was that fighting, whipping, sweating and blackened was the aristocrat of the region who owned several logging camps, a general store and lots of property. Up to this time he was a man of note, who for one thing a short time before, had for his guest Buffalo Bill. He went by the title of Captain T. J. La Flesh. Well I remember when we were in the fiercest of the battle with the flames I dipped a pail full of water to throw on the flames – muddy from the creek. He said, "Good!" and tried to drink it. I hurried to the house to get drinking water.

Thus, the ground where a short time before stood a most beautiful forest of pine trees was now a large acreage of blackened stumps."

Myron mentioned pastimes when he was young, and one of them was swimming in the creek. He also talked about building dugout canoes out of old pine logs leftover from a logging camp to the north. Partridge were common in Sherwood in Myron's early days. He hunted them often and aimed for the head. Next he wrote about some of his favorite hunting stories while living in Sherwood Forest.

A BUCK THAT NEARLY KICKED ME – "Thinking back over the hunting incidents of my life, one stands out by far above all others because of the combination of so many strange things happening all at once. It happened one day when my dad planned a drive and my uncle and I were to take our stand on two crossings on the Washburn Farm

Road while he made a drive from the east. We had just got to the first crossing and were deciding who would stand here and which of us would go to the next, when suddenly from the west, running at full speed, a large buck broke from the woods. I seemed to be exactly in his path and there was just a second's time to cock both barrels of my gun loaded with buckshot, throw it to my shoulder, and pull the trigger of the right barrel, only to have it snap and fail to fire. Fortunately both barrels being cocked, I pulled the second trigger when he was about one jump away and jumped to one side. The buck, when shot at such close range was killed so dead that he keeled a somersault and struck on his back where I had stood.

This all happened so quick that neither of us got excited until it was all over. Then we began to wonder how come and what does all this mean, when along came a bunch of hounds, which accounted for his hurry. But another strange problem we wanted answered – where was he hit that should cause such sudden death? We couldn't find a mark anywhere on his whole body, but at least Uncle said, "There's blood coming out of his mouth so we opened his mouth and found the whole charge of buckshot had gone in without even touching the surrounding skin.

Of course the owners of the hounds were soon with us and for their part wanted that head for mounting, so we gave it to them."

MYRONS THOUGHTS ON HIS SCHOOL DAYS – "Though the story of my school days was not always one of success or accomplishment, it was owing to other things besides dumbness.

When the class of my age in one school went into the fourth grade, the school I had been attending was just going into third grade. To go along with the other class I had to skip a grade. I never, according to my memory, got any personal attention from a teacher and to this day I don't see how I ever accomplished a reasonable education, but figure it came about for one thing by watching the classes above me in their class recitations and getting old enough to see the importance of education and working hard later on..."

THE WINTER I WAS 13 or 14 – "That winter I was hardly man enough to do a man's work so my dad let me do chores and haul dinner on a hand sled to the men working two miles away in the woods. There I made a fire and made a kettle of coffee for their dinner.

I enjoyed that winter very much for I tied a rifle on the sled and every day was a hunting day for it so happened that there were snowshoe rabbits everywhere. I got one or more every day and they were just as white as the snow itself so that sometimes I would discover them by seeing only the eye. I made it a practice to shoot at the eye and I guess I succeeded fairly well for the men marveled that every rabbit's head had practically been shot off, it being a 45-60 rifle I was using.

It was that winter I killed my first deer. I heard the sawyers say they saw a deer about every day and hearing that just about gave me the buck fever. Soon after hearing about it I inquired of the men where they had seen it last. One day they had seen it right near where they had left to come to dinner, so after dinner I went out according to their direction and sure enough, there stood a large buck, the likes of which I had never seen before. I drew bead and fired but he didn't drop dead like the rabbits I had been shooting and I followed him quite a ways, but didn't find one drop of blood on the snow. It surely was ridiculous. I could have shot a rabbit's eye and here I missed a whole deer!

Well I got really concerned about myself and went right about to find the reason… My failure was not that I didn't know how to shoot but I had to find out why I missed that deer, so I took a stump about the distance away as the deer was, and put a mark on the center and shot with a coarse sight and found the bullet hit seven or eight inches high…

On this second try it was a horse of another color and somehow as I drew near where I was to see my quarry I began to get weak. Something was coming on me that I didn't feel before, but I had learned how I failed before and was determined it must not happen again. As I got near where I was supposed to see the deer I was feeling pretty weak. I remember my dad's advice to not shoot it through the paunch, for it would make a nasty cleaning job.

All of a sudden I saw him standing about 100 yards away and now came the test. When I came to take aim, that gun which actually weighed about 10 lbs. seemed just all I could lift and I raised it and tried several times before I was sure of my aim. I got the sight right down in the notch, the same as though shooting at a rabbit and when I pulled the trigger he fell and never got up. But what do you know? I forgot all about the paunch and that's exactly where I hit him. Some might question a stomach shot being a killing shot, but I know this deer never got up and when I got to him he was dead."

The Pickering Brothers at Sherwood Forest
L to R: Dave Sparks (Grandfather of David Haumschild from Cary Township), Myron Pickering, Dave Pickering, Earl Pickering
(Pickering Family Photo)

Myron Pickering lived out the remainder of his life near Crane, Montana, with his wife Mary (Borgers) Pickering, after leaving Sherwood in 1906. Myron and Mary raised five children together. Myron died in 1966.

Post Office History

In addition to the post office at Nevins which was established in 1879, operated at the La Flesh homestead, and continued until 1904 by the Pickering family, there were four other post offices in Sherwood's early days. Irene, established in 1902 at the residence of Leon Campbell, was located on the northwest edge of the township near the Washburn border. Irene Post Office existed just two years, closing in 1904.

Brook Post Office was located in the heart of the township next to the town hall. Thomas Sparks was postmaster and this post office also operated from 1902 to 1904.

Popple was an early post office that served the residents of southern Sherwood Forest from 1880 until 1884 and was located in Section 25. Its first postmaster was Ben Seeley and later, Isaac Meddaugh, the man who was shot by Hugh Perkins.

Dewhurst Post Office was located in the south half of the township in Section 26 with John L. Sullivan as first postmaster in 1887, taking over the area served by the former Popple Post Office. After a few years of closure, Mr. Sullivan started the Dewhurst P.O. back up in 1895 and it lasted until 1926 as Sherwood Township's longest running post office. In 1908 the yearly salary of the Dewhurst postmaster was $64.

Dewhurst School and Dewhurst Post Office were named for Richard Dewhurst, a lumberman, attorney, banker, and politician who lived in Neillsville, Wisconsin. A township in southwestern Clark County was also named for Mr. Dewhurst.

Original Nevins Postmark on an envelope from 1901 addressed to the Pickering Family (Author's Photo)

Early 1900s

The Lutheran Sunday School held church services in the town hall on Sunday afternoons in 1900. Another group pitched tents near the town hall for revival meetings at this time with services led by traveling preachers. Dances were also held at the town hall in the early 1900s. Another event held at the hall were meetings for the Farmers' Institute with men of note coming to the community to speak. In 1903 the township purchased four dozen new chairs, and I think some of those same chairs are still there and in use today.

In about 1903, the Herman Schwanebeck family moved from Table Rock, Nebraska, to Sherwood. They traveled by train to the station in City Point and were met by Jacob Jacobson who brought them up to Sherwood, a trip into the wilderness that frightened Herman's wife.

Herman and Amelia's children who made the move to Wisconsin were Mattie, Max, Paul and Elsie. Charlie was born later in Sherwood. The family first rented a house across from the Dewhurst School that Mr. Jacobson owned and later they fixed up a log house for themselves.

Herman Schwanebeck & Amelia (Boeck) Schwanebeck
Ancestors of the Sherwood Schwanebeck Family
(Schwanebeck Family Photos)

Sherwood Sunday School at Herman Schwanebeck Farm
(Schwanebeck Family Photo)

L to R: Paul Schwanebeck, John Fluegel, Seltrecht or Charles Gall, Mr. Wittcamp, Martha (Schwanebeck) Freedlund, Elsie (Schwanebeck) Fluegel, Theresa (Gehre) Jacobson, Conjourly, Amanda Gehre (girl in front is Bernice (Gehre) Hiles, Anna Schwanebeck (holding Irma), Amelia Schwanebeck, Seltrecht, Ella Schwanebeck holding child, Herman Schwanebeck, Wittkamp, Julius Gehre, Gall, Seltrecht, Conjourly. Four children in front of Martha Freedlund and Elsie Fluegel are possibly Freedlunds and Fluegels. (Root cellar in the background)

Elsie remembered that her mother, Amelia (Boeck) Schwanebeck, always had a large garden. They raised and butchered their own pigs, geese, and ducks, and also smoked the duck breasts. Amelia made pumpkin soup, also many coffee cakes, cookies, bread, and homemade ice cream. Sherwood neighbors came together often with potluck dinners.

Herman and Amelia Schwanebeck farmed in Sherwood and a 1913 news article mentioned Herman and his son, Max, and stated that they owned 160 acres of land in Sherwood at that time. Along with improved buildings they had 19 cows, 4 horses, and some young stock. The Schwanebecks put in 28 acres of corn and were putting up a silo in 1913. Herman's milk checks were said to run over $100. per month and the reporter noted that his hard work had paid off.

Herman and Amelia's descendants continued to farm in Sherwood and several still live and own farm land in the township yet today.

**Joe Jacobson on far right, son of Jacob Jacobson
Photographer – Taylor, Circa 1914** (Jacobson Family Photo)

John Freedlund, born in 1852 in Sweden, was the patriarch of the Freedlund family of Sherwood. John and his wife, Emma, knew each other in Sweden. John came to America first in 1876, and Emma followed in 1878, a year before they were married in Rockford, Illinois.

When John first arrived in the U.S., he located at Bishop Hill, Illinois, where a Swedish commune had started up in the 1850s. There was a large population of Swedish immigrants in Henry County, Illinois, near Bishop Hill. After a year there, John found work in furniture factories and kept at that occupation for ten years or more. He then built a home in Rockford, and later operated a farm in Avon Township, Rock County, Illinois, where he was living on the 1900 census with wife, Emma, and their seven children.

History is lost as to why John purchased land from a lumber company in Sherwood in about 1903, land that was filled with pine stumps. Stump pulling was a necessary job for many Sherwood folks with ambitions of farming. John's sons, Clarence and Allen, pulled stumps with horses and later purchased a stump puller machine. Some of the stumps left over from the logging days were over four feet in diameter.

The Freedlund family planted an orchard at their farm in Sherwood in Section 26 with sixteen varieties of apple trees, four different plum trees, cherries, and gooseberries. Their barn was built in 1929 and Allen Freedlund was not able to pay the builders after losing his savings in the Broadway Bank at Rockford, Illinois, during the stock market crash. Allen lost $2,900., money he'd made from selling his honey in Rockford.

Allen's widow, Rugna (Jacobson), and their son Donald, finally paid off the barn debt in the 1940s. The crash left so many with nothing and the struggle of having to start all over again must have been unbearable.

John Freedlund   Emma & John Freedlund
(Freedlund Family Photos)

Donald Freedlund said his mother, Rugna, had a good chicken house and bought 200 chickens. Egg money was important and sometimes the only extra spending money for a farm wife. The Freedlund family sold a cow for $11.75 in 1932. In order to pay a hospital bill the Freedlund family sold a large cow, and in order to buy a 1929 Pontiac they sold six heifers. On Allen's first drive in his new car, the first curve he attempted to navigate left him sitting in the ditch. Cars in those days were started with a hand crank and when turning the crank, Allen ended up with a blister on his hand that turned into blood poisoning and six weeks in the hospital.

One time after developing pneumonia, Allen was in the hospital for a couple of months. While he was ill, his wife hired a son-in-law of John Eggen, a neighbor to the south on County Trunk Z, to help out on the Freedlund farm. Eggen was laid off from the railroad and welcomed his pay of 50 cents a day. I think that was pretty standard pay for a farm hand at that time.

John Freedlund's sons, Clarence and Allen, both operated fine farms in Sherwood. Many of their descendants still live in the township today.

Frederick (Fritz) and Hannah Gall moved to Sherwood about 1909 from Hinton, Iowa. They farmed on the west side of County Trunk Z in Section 17. A family story is that Hannah never learned to speak English, but preferred to speak in her native German language all her life. Two of Fritz and Hannah's children married Sherwood born siblings and became lifelong residents; Albert Gall married Mayme Scholtz and Clara Gall married Ralph Scholtz. Ralph and Clara Scholtz lived out their lives on the original Scholtz farm with a frame home built in the 1880s that still stands on Highway 73 in Section 10. The Scholtz home, now owned by Theresa Mueller, may be one of the oldest homes in Sherwood.

Herman Schwanebeck at his farm with Charles Gall
(Schwanebeck Family Photo)

Receipt from Art Ziemendorf's Sherwood Corners Store
Dated July 2, 1957

Sherwood Businesses

Previously mentioned, the Wood County Manufacturing Company operated a saw mill in Section 9 on the south side of now Hwy 73. In 1888 the company purchased forty acres for their mill site for $900. from J. Reddan, a Neillsville businessman. The mill sawed white oak and red oak trees, and made shingles, staves for wooden barrels, and lumber. There were many men employed at the mill in the late 1890s. A small railroad track was laid to the north of the mill which transported slabs and lumber to the north and away from the mill. The Wood County Mfg. Company folded up in the 1890s, but the remains of a huge sawdust pile could be seen as late as the 1930s at the old mill site.

Arthur Ziemendorf pumping gas at his grocery store at "Sherwood Corners" located across from the Sherwood Town Hall – Circa 1926

In 1902 a general grocery store was built west of the town hall by James Wolbert who was busy stocking it with goods in May of that year. Years later the store was purchased by Robert and Viola Schreiber. Robert and Viola left Sherwood in 1921 after selling the store to Viola's father, Ed Ziemendorf. Ed passed the business on to his son Art, in May of 1935, after Art was discharged from his service in the C.C.C. camps, with the stipulation that Art take care of his parents.

Art Ziemendorf married Lillian Hofer and in 1947 they relocated their business from Sherwood Corners to a quarter mile north on the same side of Highway 73. Lillian said the old store was on such low ground that in wet times she had to sweep water out the door and it would pour back in just as fast as she swept it out. With her quick sense of wit Lillian joked that they were the first family in Sherwood to have running water.

The Sherwood Store was a mainstay of the community for many years. In earlier times, goods purchased most often at the store were flour, sugar, salt, cocoa, coconut, etc. One could trade eggs and butter there for merchandise. In later years a tavern was added on to the store at its new location. Dewey Ziemendorf, and later his son, Lloyd and wife, Frances who took over the store in 1960, served the community until 1973. In the 1960s I remember the DX sign by the gas pump in front of the store.

Sherwood Store on Highway 73 in 1958
(Ziemendorf Family Photo)

Another reason the Ziemendorf's relocated their store in 1947 was because this was the year that Hwy 73 was paved and the square corners became rounded corners in Sherwood. No longer did the main highway travel past the Sherwood Store and the Sherwood Town Hall.

Also, in the early 1940s, Clark Electric brought electricity to Sherwood. Lighting was the main attraction for those who hooked up with electric service. Many families had just one outlet installed on the outside of their homes. Prior to electricity, farmers used gas lamps that did give off more light than a light bulb, but the glass shades had to be cleaned often. It had been a long wait for the residents and the excitement of having electricity available was perhaps somewhat like the arrival of high speed internet to Sherwood via phone lines for us today.

The Seltrecht and Coulthard families moved to Sherwood in the spring of 1902. About this time a creamery was built next to the grocery store, along with an ice house and barn. The creamery was short lived as it burned down just four years later in 1906. It was owned by Charles Wallace at that time and luckily he had it insured for $2,300. with Lynn Mutual Insurance Company. After an investigation and a jury trial, Wallace was awarded the damages. John R. Coulthard and Dan Hill, with help from neighbors, worked hard to save the nearby grocery store from the fire that destroyed the creamery.

A small group of Sherwood farmers organized a cooperative in 1912 to build and operate a cheese factory near the town hall. They named it the Sherwood Dairy Company and the first stockholders were R. C. Schreiber, John R. Coulthard, and A. A. Gates, who lived nearby. Farmers had to haul their cream by wagon to the Pittsville Creamery after the first creamery burned down in 1906. Chris Feitz and John Voegeli were some of the first cheese makers to run the factory. Voegeli began making cheese at Sherwood in 1914 after learning the trade in Oconomowoc. He married Sherwood native, Minnie Tompson, daughter of Bertha Scholtz, in 1916, and they later moved to Cambria, Wisconsin. Several others ran the cheese factory through the years until it burned down in May of 1929, never to be rebuilt.

Frank Sholtz, Sherwood Cheese Factory (Circa late 1920s)

In August of 1912, telephone lines were completed toward Sherwood from the east. The lines ran from Pittsville out to the Town Hall. Mr. Coffee, the auctioneer, was said to be the only customer out this way to hook up a phone. He lived near the Wood/Clark County line in Sherwood and hoped a telephone would help his business.

In 1913 the press boasted that the cheese factory had as high as 3,600 pounds of milk daily during cooler weather. The factory was shipping cheese weekly from the train station at Progress, six miles to the east. The main product of the Sherwood Dairy Company was brick cheese.

Farmers from Sherwood in 1913 who were prospering were Schwanebeck, Gall, Coulthard, Eggen, Janes, Gates, Frieber, Bender and Jacobson. People from Illinois were building up new homes on Sherwood's north side according to the press.

Sherwood Corners – Circa 1916. Peter Peterson walking home with a sack of flour over his shoulder. On the left is the Sherwood Store and barn. On the right is the town hall and cheese factory.
(Ziemendorf Family Photo)

This article from the *Pittsville Record* in 1914 sums up the above photo perfectly. "The editor of this paper made a short call at Sherwood Sunday and stopping at the store of R. C. Schreiber found friend Rob smiling through the best of spirits over good fall trade. Directly across the road is the cheese factory... This factory has an enviable reputation as a maker of good cheese and the new cheesemaker, a Swiss, direct from the Alps, knows how to cater to the wants of the cheese consumer of America. The factory has had a good run this summer. Also in this little collection of buildings may be found the Sherwood town hall. Here is where all the public meetings, town meetings, dances, and other gatherings of this thrifty community are held. The country round about shows the result of labor and thrift, and many fine farms grace the undulating landscape. Sherwood is one of the best farming communities in Wisconsin and some of the best farmers live there. Crops are abundant, the weather just as though it had been ordered, sickness passes them by and the smile of contentment is on the face of the average Sherwoodite." (Do you think he was looking for subscribers?)

A tavern owned by the McCann family started up in the 1930s and was located just east of the corner of Hwy 73 and County Trunk W. Clayton McCann and later Harry Hoehne operated a fix-it shop in a garage next to the tavern. Some tavern owners at this location throughout the years were Tom and John Paun, who took the tavern over in 1946, Winnie and Andy Miller, Henry "Hank" Alsterberg, and John and Laura Bowen. I remember the tavern as, "Hank's W Inn". It was a small bar with just a few bar stools, but it had a lively atmosphere.

Paun's Tavern on Corner of 73 & W – Circa 1950

The Deer Trail Cafe began in the 1950s and was operated first by the Hanson family of Washburn Township. Later this business was sold to the Light and Bohnsack families who rented it out to Gladys Neuman, and then sold it to the Pederson family. Merle and Margaret Pederson operated the Deer Trail from about 1966 to their retirement in 1976, then keeping it for their residence.

The Deer Trail Cafe was located on Highway 73 on Sherwood's northwest side, west of Cherry Avenue. It was a welcome place for truckers traveling from the east who stopped on their commute to and from the Twin Cities. From the day the Cafe opened until the day it closed, Mary Paun worked there as cook, waitress, and dishwasher. The Pedersons opened up Sunday nights at 8 p.m. and kept their doors open twenty-four hours a day, all week, until noon on Saturday. They served homemade soups, pies, and specials of the day, and during deer season everyone had to wait in line to order their meals.

Deer Trail Cafe (Pederson Family Photo)

After the closing of Ziemendorf's store and tavern in 1973 a much needed gap was filled in the Sherwood community with the creation of Dick's Toy Banke in 1974. Dick and Frances Luther purchased a small building from Marshfield formerly used by the Tri County Bank. They remodeled the bank building and added onto it creating a tavern and small store. Frances's father, George Dibble Sr., rearranged the lettering on the outside wall of the building and spelled out the words "Toy Banke" just for fun, and the name stuck.

The Luther family were very community oriented, carrying extra supplies in their little store for neighbors, hunters, and campers at the Sherwood Park. They also sold gasoline and many locals filled up water jugs from an outside faucet in the back of the building whenever they needed it. Dick was the local fire warden and town chairman for several years. Frances catered many occasions in the basement including wedding showers and baby showers. She often baked fancy cakes for the events. The Luthers hosted annual coon feeds, bear feeds, and wild game feeds with much of the food home cooked by Frances herself. Every year Christmas parties were given for the neighbor children with Santa passing out gifts. The Toy Banke also sponsored a baseball team that played at the Granton Park.

Dick's Toy Banke Bar & Store - Circa 1975
(Luther Family Photo)

When Dick and Frances retired they sold their business to Randy and Connie Reshel who renamed it, R & C Roadhouse. The Roadhouse tavern still serves the community well today, offering great food, including a Friday night fish fry.

Churches

St. Paul's Evangelical Lutheran Church was established at Sherwood in 1925 but for more than twenty years prior to this, Lutherans from Sherwood met in their homes and at the town hall. Officers elected at St. Paul's first meeting at the home of Fred Rennhack in Sherwood were: Reinhold Wittkamp, chairman; Paul Schwanebeck, secretary; and Albert Knoll, treasurer. Trustees elected were: Reinhold Wittkamp, Herman Schwanebeck, and Albert Knoll. The congregation purchased an acre of land to build their church on in December of 1925 from Albert and Mayme Gall east of the town hall. Early church members met at the Sherwood town hall until the church was built in 1932. Construction was supervised by Otto Roessler of Chili and labor was provided by church members. The building has been remodeled through the years but the original portion built in 1932 still remains. A basement was built under the original church in 1953.

One year in the 1950s, on Easter Sunday, the gravel roads in Sherwood were not drivable by car. The Schwanebeck families loaded up trailers pulled by their tractors to make it to church service that day. Rev. A. H. Moog, pastor, thought there would be very few attending but he was pleasantly surprised at the dedication of the members.

Lutheran Sunday School was taught on Sunday mornings before church services for many years as well as catechism classes for children preparing for their confirmation.

The Sherwood Lutheran Ladies Aide still meets monthly and has provided a great service to the community for many years by serving meals for Sherwood family funerals. St. Paul's Lutheran Church shares their pastor with St. John's Lutheran Church in Pittsville.

St. Paul's Lutheran Church - 2015
(Author's Photo)

Early records, handwritten by Myron Pickering, mention the organization of a religious class at Sherwood in 1892 with leadership by Mr. Reverend Scott from the Pittsville M. E. Church. Classes continued under Methodist control until prominent members became dissatisfied in 1898. Rev. John Willan and Rev. Longenecker then helped to tie loose ends and organize a Sunday School at Sherwood that met at the town hall. Names of members active in this early organization were Sparks, Pickering, Messing, and St. Germain. These families created the foundation that set the stage for a second church to be built in Sherwood just east of the town hall in 1936 that was known as the Sherwood Community Church.

Mrs. George (Sadie) Redman and her husband moved to the area in 1922 from Chicago and spearheaded the plans to build the church. Sadie and several other women were elected as officers and the following joined as charter members: Mrs. Ed. Ziemendorf, Mrs. John Coulthard, Mrs. Ralph Lawson, Mrs. Albert Gall, and Mrs. P. L. Reisse. Together they formed "The Sherwood Community Club" with the purpose of fund raising to eventually build a church. The club held suppers and sold greeting cards, cookbooks, magazine subscriptions, and vanilla to raise funds. They also held chicken pie suppers at the town hall. This late summer event became popular far and wide and by 1936 they had the funds to build.

Later charter members of the club were: Mrs. A. M. Blakely, Mrs. Ralph Scholtz, Mrs. Oscar Brinkmeier, Miss Flora Janes, Mrs. Art Gehre, and Mrs. Mosier.

Tickets for the Annual Chicken Pie Dinner Fund Raiser

In 1958, six church pews were purchased by the Sherwood Community Church for $12.00 from St. Paul's Lutheran Church.

The Sherwood Community Church was torn down in 1996 after many members had passed on or moved away and the church foundation was in disrepair. The last remaining officer was Lydia Schafer, treasurer, who kept the church records faithfully until the end.

Browsing through those early records that survived from the late 1930s through the mid-1950s I learned that Otto Roessler from Chili was also the carpenter who built the Community Church.

Sherwood Community Church - Circa 1996
(Ziemendorf Family Photo)

Theresa Moeller Mallory said she remembered walking to the town hall for church services in the early 1930s with her parents and siblings. They were renting a farm about a half mile south on County Z at that time. Her mother would wrap pennies in a hanky for her young daughters to drop in the collection plate during the service.

A Community Club, with members from both churches in Sherwood, took turns meeting in members' homes and on May 21, 1952, at the home of Mrs. Ralph Lawson the following ladies were in attendance with their children: Leta Jacobson, Mrs. Chester (Lois) Freedlund, Mrs. Pederson, Mrs. Todd, Miss Sparks, Eleanor Coulthard, Mrs. John Coulthard, Betty Fluegel, Mrs. John Fluegel, Alma Rennhack, Mrs. George Florence Sr., Gloria Florence, Clara Scholtz, Olga Moeller, Lillian Ziemendorf, Mrs. Chapman, Donnie Freedlund, Mrs. Hanson, and Lydia Schafer.

Sherwood Cemetery

Records are few concerning the Sherwood Cemetery. A town ledger from 1882 has an entry of when the township hired Stillman Ellis to fix up the "burying ground" but it is unclear what location these notes refer to. The one half acre mentioned, was to be cleared of all brush, logs, roots, and stumps, which were to be burned on the cemetery grounds. The land was also to be plowed, dragged and seeded down. A good board fence was to be built around it with white oak posts set two feet in the ground. Stillman Ellis won the bid on the job and was paid $38.00 for his work.

C. S. Stockwell, surveyor, plotted out the *Sherwood Forest Cemetery*, as the map dated 1896 calls it, in the location the cemetery is at today. A row along the north side of the original plot was taken over by State Highway 73 though, and never used for burials.

In 1898 the town board set fees for purchasing cemetery lots, asking $3.00 for choice lots and $2.00 for inferior lots, with payment required before a burial. During the same month in 1898, the board agreed to hire Joseph Janes to move three bodies from the old grave yard to the new one with the town paying those expenses. Remains moved were those of the Stillman Ellis family - his wife Henrietta, their son, and daughter. Joseph Janes, who took on the job, was Stillman's son-in-law. The three Ellis family members had been previously buried on land owned by Stillman Ellis in Section 14, on a knoll near Adam Moeller's log cabin across the road and on the north side of Hwy 73 from where the cemetery is today. This may have been the "burying ground" referred to in 1882.

Town records also mention moving two more bodies to the Sherwood Cemetery in 1910 from private property in the township. One was a Seltrecht infant who had been buried in the yard of the Seltrecht family property. The other was Daniel Chapman Perkins, the Civil War veteran, and father of Hugh Perkins. Daniel's remains now lie near the Unknown Soldier's gravestone.

In 1927, school teacher, Esther Sharp Dodte, when walking from the home she boarded at to Birdland Echo where she taught, had a frightening cemetery story to tell. A Sherwood resident committed suicide after three different attempts to finish the deed and had recently been buried in the cemetery. A large mound of dirt still sat next to his grave. As Esther walked past, early in the morning, a huge dog appeared to leap out of the fresh grave. Her heart sank, thinking the poor man had just returned to earth as a dog. She ran the rest of the way to the school house and didn't look back. Esther never forgot this incident as she recounted it to me over sixty years later.

For years, the identity of the Unknown Soldier in Sherwood Cemetery was a mystery. Records were found last year from 1938 when Frank Sholtz, Sherwood Town Clerk, applied to the Veteran's Administration for a gravestone, for a Civil War veteran he only knew from the old cemetery map as "McCormick". To obtain a gravestone for a veteran the government requires certain information including both first and last names, along with the state and company they served with, if a Civil War veteran. Since Frank's application lacked the requested information, the state simply furnished a stone with the words "Unknown Soldier" inscribed on it.

Several years ago an obituary was found in an old newspaper on microfilm for Patrick McCormick from 1884 that mentioned his burial at Sherwood and stated he was one of Sheridan's Scouts. With further research it was learned his full name was Charles Patrick McCormick who fought for Michigan during the Civil War and was indeed one of Sheridan's Scouts. McCormick had been employed as a logger at Scranton, east of City Point, in 1880, had family in Waushara County like so many other early settlers, and most likely died from tuberculosis. This more detailed information allowed us to order a gravestone for McCormick, years before learning that he was actually the veteran with the Unknown Soldier's stone.

Daniel Perkins and Charles McCormick both now have gravestones obtained from the Veteran's Administration and in fact, Charles McCormick has two.

John R. Coulthard lived across the road from the town hall and had a pair of black horses he attached to a buckboard and used as a hearse for Sherwood funerals. He transported the deceased from the town hall where services were held, before the churches were built, to the cemetery. Grant Coulthard, John's son, said the road from their farm to the cemetery was a corduroy road in those early days, made up of tamarack trees lying horizontally across the roadway so one could get through the mud. He said in times other than winter when the road was snow packed, everyone's last ride was a bumpy one.

A photo of the cemetery from about 1920 showed the cemetery grounds as rather unkempt with tall weeds growing around the gravestones. At some point the town board began hiring locals to mow the grounds and keep it in beautiful condition as it is today. Marla Martin remembers helping her grandfather, Adam Moeller, who mowed the cemetery for many years with a reel mower. In the early 1950s Marla would pick up the metal stakes that marked the lot corners as Adam mowed around them and then she'd put the stakes back in place. Grandpa would tell her stories that he remembered about the different folks resting there.

Grave digging was a thankless job that needed to be done in all seasons and neighbors took on the task whenever needed. Digging through frozen ground and tree roots with shovels and picks often made the task overwhelming. Since early records were not kept well occasionally a grave digger would run into an old grave while digging a new grave. In 1969, while two men were digging a grave near the middle of the cemetery they came across something unusual. An old wooden casket was encountered, but it was turned the wrong way, facing north and south rather than east and west, as is traditional. The grave was near that of the Unknown Soldier and it was thought that this may have been an old veteran's grave. We can only guess why this coffin was placed in an untraditional way or who it belonged to. There are many unmarked graves in Sherwood Cemetery.

Seven men who fought in the Civil War and thirty-six veterans who served during WWI, WWII, Korea, the Vietnam era, and in Peace Time are buried at Sherwood Cemetery. We are thankful to have local veterans from the Pittsville area and the Pittsville High School Band hold a service at the Sherwood Cemetery each Memorial Day morning to honor all who served.

Sherwood Cemetery, Backside of the Gravestone of Magnus Moe, a young child who died in 1892 - Circa 1905 (Fields Collection)

Fun Times in Early Days

Schwanebeck Kids on the Farm (Schwanebeck Family Photo)

Sherwood Boys on Bikes, Late 1920s - L to R: Iver & Lawrence Freedlund, Glenn Schwanebeck, Carl Anderson   (Schwanebeck Family Photo)

In February of 1915, the press announced that moving picture shows were to be presented at the Sherwood Town Hall on a weekly basis. I'm not sure how long the movies were shown but I can imagine the excitement this created.

Barn dances in Sherwood were held in the 1930s in the loft of Henry Seltrecht's new barn. Their first barn burned down in 1932 along with almost half of their dairy herd. After the new barn was built, designed by Otto Roessler of Chili, Seltrecht applied for a liquor and cigarette license from Town of Sherwood. He had high hopes of making sales during the dances which were held every Sunday night. On a malt beverage license from 1935, Henry said he'd be selling the goods in the "east room on the second floor" of his barn.

Local bands played music for barn dances all across the Midwest during the '30s. Names of some groups who played music at Sherwood were the Klarisch Orchestra of Greenwood, the Melbrecht Family Orchestra of Pittsville, and The Six Badger Aces of Abbotsford. Many of the band members signed their names on the walls inside the Seltrecht barn. Charges for admission to the dances in 1934 were 35cents for men but ladies got in free. Seltrecht also showed a few movies in his Sherwood barn.

On the 4th of July in 1934, Henry hosted an all-day event at his barn and "grove" as advertised in the newspaper. The event was to have motorcycle, foot, fat man, and sack races with prizes given. Lunches were to be served all day and night with dancing in both the afternoon and the evening. Some of the advertised contests that day involved nail driving and cracker eating. In the evening dance on the 4th of July, noise makers, hats, confetti, and horns were passed out to the crowd.

Another pastime in Sherwood during the 1930s was listening to the radio but not every home had one. An invitation from a neighbor to come and listen to a show, a boxing match, or to "hear the fights", was welcomed.

Seltrecht Barn - Owned today by Greg & Laura Prewitt
Circa 2003   (Author's photo)

Theresa Mallory pleasantly recalled her young days in the late 1930s with the Sherwood 4-H club. She said in about 1938 the 4-H leader for the girls was Josephine Coulthard and the leader for the boys was George Florence, Sr. The group met at the Sherwood Town Hall. Some activities she remembered doing were learning to sew special projects and cutting out dresser scarves from oil cloth. The Sherwood 4-H boys planted trees and learned about gardening.

The sport of hunting has always been a fun pastime in Sherwood. In January of 1938, what was called the Big Central Wisconsin Fox and Wolf Hunt was to take place. The Sportsmen's Club of Central Wisconsin, a group of over 60 men and women organized at Marshfield, who hoped to promote conservation, headed the hunt. The group's president was from Loyal. The purpose of the hunt was to cut down the wolf, fox, and bobcat population in a twelve mile radius of Sherwood Township and help out the game bird population in Sherwood where birds were known to thrive. Hunters coming to the Sunday event were to meet at Pittsville and carry shotguns only, loaded with nothing larger than No. 2 shot. It was publicized in the local press with much enthusiasm with Sherwood as the hunter's destination.

Ivan Schwanebeck with Fox in 1950s (Schwanebeck Family Photo)

The Depression

The stock market crash in 1929 left folks who had savings in local banks with nothing and Sherwood's residents did not escape those devastating times.

A 1930 assessment roll for the town of Sherwood lists personal property in much more detail than today and gives us an interesting glimpse into the changing modes of transportation and types of animals on the farm. There were 43 autos or trucks in the township that year. Livestock was also taxed and those listed on the statement of assessment in 1930 were 104 horses, 633 cattle, 85 sheep, 23 pigs, and 77 wagons, carriages or sleighs. Not every family owned an automobile and some from that era, like my grandfather, never learned to drive a car.

Axel Moeller shared a few stories about Sherwood in the 1930s with some tidbits about his own family life during that time frame. It was a hard, hard decade. One in which the Great Depression continued really until the start of World War II. Axel said his father, Adam Moeller, rented a few different farms in the early 1930s while he worked at improving his own eighty acres, building a home there for his family. He rented the Ed Ziemendorf home for $5.00 a month in Section 24.

When the Adam Moeller family lived on the Mosier place on Todd Road, Grandpa worked for a widow he called the honorable Mrs. Redman, grubbing out stumps at her farm (later known as the Bert Todd Farm). His pay was fifty cents per day plus a quart of milk as a bonus. Adam's family ate dandelion greens when spring came and suckers and redhorse they caught in the East Fork of the Black River at the end of Todd Road.

A Day's Small Catch in 1932 – Earl and Cecil Moeller on Todd Road with the fish they caught in the East Fork of the Black River in Sherwood.
(Moeller Family Photo)

During these rough times, Uncle said any money was good money. Many of the school kids trapped skunks, muskrat, mink, and weasels, checking their trap lines early in the morning before school started. Sometimes they came to school smelling like skunks. Beaver were hard to find during the depression, most had been trapped out of the area. Overalls cost $3.00 a pair. Beer was sold in half gallon bottles called G-bottles and cost 25 to 50 cents a bottle.

Along with the Depression, after the stock market crash of '29, came droughts in the 1930s and fires started up south of Sherwood in the peat bogs of City Point. In May of 1934, a fire swept from near Pray, Wisconsin, into southwestern Wood County, burning eastward on an eighteen mile long path. Although some fires were put out, they continued to burn in the rich peat soil for several years without any way to extinguish them.

During this horrific time of drought, wells near houses and barns went dry. With little hay to feed their cattle, farmers led their livestock to lower Sherwood ground so they could feed on marsh grass still growing and green.

Donald Freedlund told how they would drive their cattle to the East Fork of the Black River twice a day for water to drink. William Bodtke witched wells and was confident he could help find water. He pinpointed a spot west of Allen Freedlund's barn, along the woods, with his witching stick. Donald and Harold dug down on the marked location about seven feet. In three or four days they had all the water they needed. This was in about 1934, the same timeframe that a large wild fire swept toward Sherwood from the south.

Harold Freedlund and his sister, Ellen, could see the fire coming and went to gather up their cows from the East Fork that day. As Donald and his mother stood on their porch watching the smoke come closer they prayed, and it began to rain. Allen was down at City Point at that time fighting the fire and the flames stopped just before reaching their property east of Chester Freedlund's farm.

At times, during the droughts during the early 1930s, the air was filled with dust from the plowed fields, and erosion also became an issue. Trees were planted for wind breaks and fire lanes were created for access into remote wooded areas to aid in halting fires.

A few men from Sherwood joined the Civilian Conservation Corp in the mid to late 1930s. The closest camp to Sherwood was located just east of City Point on the north side of Highway 54. It is difficult now to learn the names of those Sherwood men who served in camps but a few of them were Oscar Larson, Lawrence W. Freedlund, Wilbur Fields, Dick Rennhack, Arthur Ziemendorf, and Cecil Moeller. Cecil Moeller served in various camp locations in northern Wisconsin near Perkinstown and Hayward. Wilbur Fields was at Camp Globe.

The standard pay for those in the C.C.C. was $25.00 per month, with $20.00 sent home to help support the inductee's family. At times, this monthly check was the main source of income for the family back at home. Camp life was somewhat like military life. Young men were required to make their beds, scrub their own laundry, and do kitchen duty. They were given uniforms, often leftovers from World War I. The C.C.C. boys dug ditches, planted trees, fought fires when needed, built roads, dams, and various other structures. Seventeen was the age for acceptance after passing a physical, but some lied about their age and entered at sixteen to help out their hungry families back home. That was the case with my father who worked in camps in Iowa.

In 1933, President Roosevelt organized the Works Progress Administration, W.P.A., to create public works jobs for the unemployed. There were no jobs in Sherwood and at that time venison was hard to come by. One project where men found employment in Sherwood through the W.P.A. was digging out road ditches along Highway 73. Several men worked at this job with nothing but shovels.

A look at the 1940 census truly shows how farming was the mainstay in Sherwood. Of fifty-seven households counted, fifty were supported by farming. The heads of household of those that were engaged in farming were: Albert Knoll, Max Falk, John Eggen, Paul Schwanebeck, Joseph Cowgill, Clarence Freedlund, Allen Freedlund, Francis Jacobson, Joe Jacobson, Charles Schwanebeck, Reuben Fields, Fred Gall, William and Louis Bodtke, Norman Freedlund, Arthur Sparks, Flora Janes and Jesse Sparks, Dewey Ziemendorf, George Florence Sr., Harry Rennhack, Arthur Gehre, Gust and Frank Palm, John Bowman, John Fluegel, Elery Messing, Adam Moeller, John R. Coulthard, Walter Hanson, Albert Gall, Edward Lindquist, Andrew B. Todd, George Fluegel, George R. Cary, Rose Seman, Ralph Scholtz, Susie McCann, Henry Seltrecht, William Camp, Melvin Galbreath, Fred Ferguson, Thomas Paun, Joseph Matonich, Steve Rosandich, Charles Marek, John Paun, Joseph Rosandich, John Martin, Oscar Larson, and Fred Hoppe.

The only two businesses in Sherwood from the 1940 census were country grocery store operator, Ed Ziemendorf, and tavern keeper/bartender, Clayton McCann.

Just a few had jobs as construction laborers: Harold Vanderhoof, Oswald Henninger, Louis Peron, and Frank McPherson. Elaine Todd, Helen Sparks, and Rose Rosandich taught school and Earl Moeller, was listed as a McNess salesman. Earl said he couldn't make a go of it selling McNess products (similar to Watkins) because so many people charged orders and never paid their bills.

Tom Paun drove the milk truck in Sherwood for many years. He lived on Sherwood's northwest side. In wintertime when side roads were snow filled, Paun would gather up milk with a team of horses and sled and haul it out to Highway 73 where his truck was parked. Many people caught a ride with Tom in his milk truck to get to town or home, especially students from Sherwood going to high school who boarded in town and teachers hoping to go home for a few days when their school had a break. Paun's daily trips were so important to the livelihood of Sherwood farmers and others who had no other form of transportation. The milkman could always be counted on.

Tom Paun – Sherwood Milk Man, in Front of the Oscar Brinkmeier Home on Highway 73 in Sherwood
(Scholtz Family Photo)

Sherwood Lake – A Grand Idea!

A Recent Photo of Sherwood Lake – (Carin Schalla Photo)

In the late 1800s, there were three logging dams on Hay Creek, known in early days as Hay Meadow Creek, in Sherwood. The future sight of the Sherwood Lake was at a location of one of those dams in Section 34.

In 1882, Niram H. Withee had four logging camps on Hay Meadow Creek and in 1883, Island Mill Lumber Company of La Crosse, worked to improve the creek by booming both sides and straightening the course of the stream. Island Mill's main headquarters were at La Crosse but they had a small office at Pray in the 1880s.

Island Mill/Bright & Withee logging camp was located where Sherwood Park is today. A sawmill operated there in the latter 1890s or early 1900s. Jacob Jacobson worked as a cook at the camp there. A huge sawdust pile from the mill also remained for many years at this location. Merlin Jacobson remembered going as a young boy with his father to gather sawdust there each year. Sherwood families used the sawdust to insulate their ice houses.

The Clark County Press mentioned the beginning of the dam construction to create Sherwood Lake in September of 1935. B. Wallace and family were said to be camping on the Janes farm while Wallace was to act as foreman of the dam's construction that fall.

Sherwood Town Chairman, John Fluegel, spoke with M. E. Wilding, Secretary of the Clark County Drainage District in October of 1935 to enquire about the construction. Fluegel was a member of the Clark County Zoning Committee. The committee arranged to meet with a work relief director from Madison to discuss the project. The Works Progress Administration organized the work effort, employing several local men on the job.

In March of 1936, Tom Paun drove to Black River Falls to haul some supplies out to Sherwood for the dam project. The community was all a buzz about the idea of having a lake of their own. In addition to a new Caterpillar D4 dozer brought in for the excavation, men also used horses that pulled earth movers to remove dirt from the lake bed. The project took a few years but was completed by 1938. About this same time, C.C.C. crews were planting red pine trees near the area where Sherwood Park is today.

A letter from Cecil Moeller, of Sherwood, to his sister, Lydia, dated July 5, 1938 mentions Sherwood Lake. "…Sunday the 3rd of July, Fred Enfield and I went to Hatfield, Neillsville, and to the W. P. A. dam down by Max Schwanebeck where the dam used to be on Hay Creek. It's quite a place now. They even have it stocked with fish already. Arlo Lawson caught a pickerel 19 ½ inches long last week below the dam…" Another letter dated the same day from Cecil's younger brother, Axel, also to Lydia, talked about the lake as well. "Day before yesterday I went down to Sherwood's dam. I went swimming there and there was a boat there so Glenn and Irene and I and Mr. [Oscar] Brinkmeier pulled it out and dumped the water out then we each took a turn paddling it out on the lake, it was sure fun and it was way over my head. Yesterday me and Cecil went swimming and if it wasn't raining this morning we would go fishing and swimming too..." On the back of the letter Axel, aged 11, sketched a pencil drawing of the dam and the lake. Next to his picture he wrote, "It's a grand thing! It's a swell place!" It must have been quite an exciting time for the local kids to explore the new lake.

Building Sherwood Dam, Circa 1935 – L to R: Glenn Brinkmeier, Bill Sunderman, Amanda Brinkmeier, Irma Sunderman. Children standing in the water: Irene Brinkmeier, Mildred Scholtz.   (Brinkmeier Family Photo)

In wintertime kids would ice skate on Sherwood Lake and up the Hay Creek channel that feeds it. Cecil Moeller, in January of 1940, had this to say, "We had a quite a few skating parties down by Max Schwanebecks where they built a big W.P.A. dam for fish preservation, etc. It's pretty big, covers about 20 acres, I mean the ice. Dot and Maxine Falk, Harold and Ellen and Donald Freedlund, Irene and Glenn Brinkmeier, Lawrence Freedlund and the rest of them that were in Sherwood, Elaine Todd, she is a school teacher now and the rest of the Todds, some boys and girls from Shortville and West Cary were there too... and Dewey Ziemendorf's kids..."

When Donald Freedlund was young, he and a cousin drove out on the ice at Sherwood Lake in a Model T Ford. The ice was supposed to be safe, but it wasn't. No one was hurt but the car broke through and sunk. They waited until spring and pulled the car out with a cable.

Lillian Ziemendorf told how ice was harvested at Sherwood Lake in the late 1930s and perhaps even later. She said the job was usually done in January, after a long cold spell. A farmer with a team of horses and a couple of men would cut up the ice on the lake with a special "ice saw". The ice blocks were cut into two foot square blocks and packed in sawdust in ice houses. The Sherwood Store most likely had its own ice house. Lillian said when ice was needed you had to dig it out of the ice house and wash off the sawdust. Then the ice block was placed in the ice box, pre-refrigerator days, and kept in a tray with a hole in the bottom to allow the water to drain out. At Ziemendorf's store they kept milk, sausage, cheese, butter, pop, and beer in the ice box. Sherwood Lake was not only important for sporting but also for refrigeration in its early years.

When the auxiliary spillway at the lake washed out in the 1940s, Donald Freedlund remembered going there and gathering up a huge bunch of northerns and taking them home. There were more fish than could be eaten so the extra ones were fed to the chickens. It wasn't long though, until the eggs tasted fishy.

In the winter of 1961-1962, the Neillsville and Southern Clark County Sportsman's Clubs together paid $700. for equipment to aerate the lake and help prevent fish freeze outs in winter time. They used two concrete cemetery vaults for housing to protect an electric 1/3 h.p. air compressor attached to 2000 feet of plastic hose weighted down with lead. Holes were punched into the hose about every 4 inches, and when plugged in, the makeshift aerator opened up a large area of water in the frozen lake in a short time.

The sports clubs also stocked the lake with large northerns after the lake was shocked to rid it of rough fish years ago. Through the years both the DNR and sporting clubs have also stocked the lake with pan fish, perch, bass, and even muskies at one time.

An electric aerator has been maintained by the Southern Clark County Sportsman's Club in more recent years. The club has held ice fishing contests at Sherwood Lake for many years on the last Sunday in February as a fund raiser and fun time for all. Years ago polka music would play over a speaker system at the "Fisheree" that was also used to broadcast the names of raffle ticket prize winners all afternoon long.

At this writing, Sherwood Lake is empty due to a failure of the auxiliary spillway in February of 2014 and structural damage to the main dam. Clark County Forestry & Parks, along with many individuals, businesses, and clubs from the surrounding area are fundraising with plans to repair the dam and give the lake more depth in the coming year so that this remote and beautiful lake can be enjoyed by future generations to come.

Sherwood Lake Catch – 1969
L to R: Wayne, Ivan, Herb, Charlie, Randy   (Schwanebeck Family Photo)

**Early Shelter House at Sherwood Lake
Cramer Horse Trail Ride** – Circa 1962
(Schwanebeck Family Photo)

War Time - How We Coped

World War II saw many young men from Sherwood join up in service of their country, with several enlisting in the Navy. Steve and Katherine Rosandich of Sherwood had four sons; Joe, John, Steve, and Thomas, enter, with their fifth son, Louie, joining near the war's end. Two more Rosandich sons, Murph and Nick, served during the Korean War. One cannot imagine the sacrifices this family made to our country and the worries that Steve and Katherine endured. Their son, John, was severely wounded in Italy.

While Sherwood families waited for letters home during war time, often in the form of censored V-Mail, those left behind coped the best they could. Elery Messing lived at the end of Lone Pine Road in Sherwood, now called Blueberry Road. The old logging dam on Tom's Creek used to have a deep hole of water that the locals fished in and called "Messing's Hole" after Elery and his family. There was a trail from the end of Blueberry Road that you could even drive a Model T on, right down to the creek years ago, according to Lloyd Ziemendorf. People used to occasionally catch large northern pike in Tom's Creek and in the East Fork of the Black River in Sherwood, as late as the 1950s.

A letter Elery Messing wrote to his daughter Roselyn in the summer of 1942 tells of his days harvesting fruit near his Sherwood farm and more. "I'm going to tell you about the time I had Saturday. I started out on this side of the river looking for berries. I thought I could cross the river anywhere above the barn but found nothing but water on the river bottom so I had to either go back to the dam or go out to 73 and cross on the bridge. I chose the latter and turned in at the old Fields house and followed the fence east and I ran into a nice patch of blackberries. I picked them, then I ate my lunch and then it clouded up. I left my thermos bottle there and went to my other patch about 15 rods from there by that time it was raining. Then I thought of my thermos bottle. I started back after it. I left my pails hanging in a tree. I looked for an hour for the first patch for my thermos bottle. I finally found it. I then started for my other patch again, that took me another hour and when I finally found the patch where I hung the pails the sun came out and I knew where I was again. I picked over 12 quarts that day. Yesterday I picked 15 quarts; today I canned them and baked bread and picked my pickles all by three o'clock... Now I am watching the cows on the meadow until they get filled up. I got a ½ can of milk a day... I guess I could pick 3 hundred quarts in my 4 patches that I got all by my own self so far. Elmer [Elery's son] came home last night; he is plowing for Lindquists today. They are paying $6.00 a day for raking cranberries this year. They will start raking Sept. 1st. I got 70 quarts of blackberries canned now. I had 55 lbs. of pickles yesterday. I am going to pick pickles every day now. I think I will get more out of them. They pay $3.25 for No. 1s, and $1.25 for No. 2s, and third grade $1.00 per 100.... I will close with love", from Daddy and Elmer.

That's what you call living off the land. And that is just what many Sherwood folks were doing sixty years ago. Elery also picked and made jelly and jam from elderberries and apples.

Roseyln wrote that back then half the food a family ate was home grown. Families grew all their own vegetables and put them up for the winter and canning was a long hot job that lasted all summer long. Beans, both string and wax, and pickles were cash crops many grew for the canning factory. Roselyn had this to say about those important crops. "After the backbreaking hours of hoeing and weeding until the plants started bearing, there were the endless hours spent picking them. Cucumbers had to be picked in the morning because you couldn't pick beans until the dew was off... You picked standing up until your back was breaking then went down on your knees and crawled along. When it seemed like you couldn't pick another bean you were finally finished – and time to go to the weighing station at Sherwood Corners. There the pickles were run over a sorter made of wooden slats and the results were weighed – so many cents per pound for the tiniest ones, the most desirable... anything bigger than [a number three] you could take home for the pigs..."

As for the bean crop, if frost was late in coming in the fall of the year and the crop kept producing, like in 1941, children were kept home from school. Keeping the green beans picked was more important to the family at that time then education. If a killing frost waited until

October, kids welcomed the start of school to get a break from chores at home.

Lillian Ziemendorf said that her husband, Art, was very busy during pickle and bean harvest time at Sherwood. After pickles were brought to the station which Art maintained by the Sherwood Store, he'd have them hauled to Pittsville where the Heinz pickle station was located. The pickles would have to be put in brine right away to prevent their spoilage. Art was kept up for long hours during pickle season, sometimes he didn't return home to Sherwood until the wee hours of the morning.

An interview I had with Anna Martin, wife of Ambrose Martin, gives a wonderful reflection on a county sponsored project in 1941 that took place in Sherwood at the town hall. That infamous town hall has been the site of so many different functions since it's erection in 1891.

Here are the notes I jotted down right after my interview with Anna in 1998. - During WWII cotton farmers were suffering and the federal government bought their surplus cotton to aid the farmers. Some of this cotton was brought to Wisconsin, and to Clark County. People had to meet some qualifications to join a program and make their own mattresses. Almost everyone in the Sherwood community qualified as they were "all in the same boat". At this time in the early spring of 1941, Anna and Ambrose Martin lived just west of the East Fork of the Black River on what is now called Sherwood Road.

The Sherwood Town Hall was chosen as the site for the mattress making project. About 12 to 15 families participated on the day that Anna and Ambrose came to the hall. Anna didn't recall any children being there and she thought they had taken the little ones to Paun's. A teacher was sent out to instruct everyone. They were given long needles to tie the mattresses together with, and fastened buttons on each side. The Martin's completed one mattress on that day. Families could make as many mattresses as they needed, but had to promise they would not sell the mattresses or make any kind of profit on them. Some of the people Anna remembered at the hall that day were; Mrs. Lindquist, John and Elsie Fluegel, Ralph and Nettie Lawson, George and Rose Florence, Ralph and Clara Scholtz, Helen Seman, Oscar and Amanda Brinkmeier, Adam Moeller, and others.

Thirty-six mattresses were made at the town hall. Sherwood was just one of a few townships in Clark County chosen for this project, and the first to complete it. Art and Lillian Ziemendorf also made a mattress at the town hall. Lillian said the hardest part was sewing by hand the roll around the mattress, but Art mastered it and also figured out how to do it with a sewing machine.

Years later Anna Martin recalled cutting up that mattress and making crib mattresses out of it. She also had a few other thoughts to share on the war time shortages in Sherwood. Ration stamps were given out for meat, shoes, gas for the car, tires, and sugar, among other things. They were only allowed a small amount of sugar per week, so they bought bees from Ralph Lawson. There was also a shortage of binder twine.

At the Sherwood Store, motor oil was delivered in quart jars with "V63" written on the lids. Lillian Ziemendorf saved the jars for canning and shared some of them with Anna Martin. The lids on these jars were a little different size than regular canning jars so when they quit making them it was hard to find lids to fit those jars.

Everyone in Sherwood had their own ration stamps during the war. Food shortages weren't too much of a problem because farmers had their own. Sugar was one thing that everyone had a shortage of, but when honey was available like on the Allen Freedlund farm and others, sugar wasn't missed too much as Anna mentioned. Gasoline was the hardest to come by, and also new car tires. People just didn't travel much by car then.

In the late 1940s, State Highway 73 was blacktopped and the square corners were removed leaving Sherwood Township with its four famous curves.

Post World War II

Although World War II was over, after a few years of peace time, Sherwood's young men stepped up again to serve their country during the Korean War.

Army Private First Class Robert Paun, a Sherwood resident, was killed in action in North Korea, on October 20, 1952. Robert was the son of Mary Paun and the late John Paun. He attended Audubon grade school and Granton High School. PFC Paun took his basic training at Fort Riley, Kansas, and was just 22 years old when he passed. Robert is buried in Saint Stephens Catholic Cemetery in Chili, Wisconsin.

The 1950s was yet a time of social gathering and neighbors helping neighbors in Sherwood. Farmers still teamed up together with heavy work such as threshing, sawing up firewood and lumber, and filling silos. A threshing machine would move from farm to farm as did saw rigs in the fall. Moldenhauers from rural Granton operated one of the traveling threshing machines.

Farmers would haul up saw logs and stack them up near their homes. When it was their turn to host the traveling saw rig the neighborhood women would cook a noon and evening meal for the crew and the men would saw until done or dark. The women considered their task as a sort of competition to see who could cook the best.

**Threshing Crew at Ralph Scholtz Farm
Ray Kane's Rig in 1953** (Scholtz Family Photo)

L to R: ?, ?, Louie Bodtke, Neil Coulthard, Jim McConnell?, ?, Ray Kane, Breseman, ?, Mueller, ?, Art Ziemendorf, Max Schwanebeck, ?, Ralph Scholtz, Ed Lindquist, Lawrence Freedlund, John Kane, Glenn Schwanebeck?. On Hay Wagon, L to R: ?, Ralph Lawson
(Scholtz Family Photo)

In 1954, the John Coulthard family "installed" a television set in their home and this exciting event made the local press. I would imagine a T.V. in the home for the first time was like the ability to go online via the Internet in our homes today.

After World War II there were still few employment opportunities in the Sherwood area for young men who did not farm at their home. They would travel to City Point to work in the cranberry marshes during the fall harvest and in summertime help with the sphagnum moss harvest. City Point was known as the moss capital of the world and like in the early logging days, Sherwood men once again headed south for work. Pulling moss was a hot miserable job, standing out in the large open marshes with no shade, and swarms of deer flies buzzing around the head and shoulders.

City Point Cranberry Harvest, 1950s
Russell Jacobson front right (Schwanebeck Family Photo)

Baling Moss at City Point, 1950s – L to R: Earl Moeller, Arvil Schafer, Unknown Man, Mr. Retzlaff

Many young men from Sherwood commuted back and forth to Rockford, Illinois, where factory and foundry jobs were plentiful. My father and uncle were two from Sherwood who worked at Drop Forge in Rockford in the 1950s commuting back and forth every weekend.

Life was difficult for wives and children home alone during the week, with their husbands gone, at work out of state. Wives were often left with no transportation. Neighbors carpooled and helped one another.

Growing cash crops continued to be an important supplement to income in the 1950s. Many families in Sherwood grew vegetables in small acreages for the local canning factory in Pittsville, which at this time was owned by Lakeside Packing Company. Farmers would sign contracts in February, and could choose to grow green beans or wax beans. Seeds were furnished by the company for twenty-five cents per pound in 1954 from the company and fertilizer could also be purchased at the same time from them. Art Ziemendorf was still taking care of the Sherwood station in the 1950s.

A contract from 1953 to purchase beans from the Pittsville canning company had this to say. "In case the factory is destroyed by the elements, or in case of strikes, riots, war, or unavoidable accidents the factory is unable to be operated, this contract is VOID. We absolutely will not accept rusty, diseased, or over-mature beans. If any such beans are found in bag, we have right to reject entire bag." The contract stressed, "Pick beans when young and tender – FREQUENTLY."

Sherwood kids enjoyed activities with the local 4-H club. Eleanor Coulthard and Theresa Mallory were 4-H leaders in the 1950s. The club met at the town hall and some activities were sewing projects and childcare for the girls. The boys learned how to make maple syrup and received blue ribbons at the Clark County Fair with their exhibits. Kids had a chance to go to 4-H summer camps near Wausau. One activity at the camp was learning to square dance and there were always campfires to sit around in the evenings.

Kids also roller skated in the town hall and had Halloween parties there too. The extra efforts of adult leadership in the community in those days helped create special memories for the Sherwood kids in the 1950s and early '60s.

With the 1960s came more local jobs in neighboring towns in factories, paper mills, and road construction. Many Sherwood men who had commuted to Illinois and Milwaukee were finally able to find work closer to home. Dairy farms were still thriving.

Deer Hunting - A Way of Life

Venison in the early days was an important supplement to meals, especially for those not living on farms. Deer meat was what helped many families make it through tough times, in season and off season. In summertime venison was eaten fresh or canned and when the needed meat ran out, someone shot another deer. Squirrel and rabbits were important for sport and food as well. When I was young we even ate the squirrel's kidneys, a real treat!

In Sherwood's early days, deer were common or certainly passed through from time to time allowing settlers like the Pickering family, to harvest plenty of venison. Deer were picked off for quick food in the logging camps and shot for sport as well. There were no laws to control the harvest and after a time the deer crop lessened, so much so that by the 1920s there were very little deer left in Sherwood, or much of the state for that matter. Donald Freedlund said he didn't see his first deer until he was about 7 or 8 years old when he caught a glimpse of a buck out the kitchen window. In 1925, the state of Wisconsin closed deer hunting season for the year and began issuing deer licenses only during even years. This policy continued until 1937 when the state opened deer season for just three days during an odd year. Gradually deer numbers picked up until the recent record harvests we've seen topping over 500,000 deer killed in the year 2000, in gun deer season alone.

With Sherwood's rich history of deer hunting, I only know about one hunting fatality that occurred in the township. From the local press and county court records, I learned that, Ingvard "Buster" Larson, died on November 6, 1935, from an apparent hunting accident. He was deer hunting with his brother, Walter, and they were crossing a small creek in the northwest part of the township near County W and Hwy 73. Buster, carrying his gun, crossed the creek first by walking on a pine stump his brother had thrown down for him. Walter handed Buster his gun and began to cross as well in the same spot. Just after he gave his gun to Buster, a shot rang out and Buster lay dead on the ground with a bullet hole in his cheek. Walter thought his gun went off in Buster's hands and quickly grabbed it, broke it, and flung it into the creek, throwing the shells out as well.

Just a couple minutes after the shot rang out another brother, Soren, who was hunting close by, came running to the scene. Walter told Soren he thought Buster had accidentally shot himself when his own gun went off just after the hand off. There was no doubt in either of their minds that Buster was dead. While Walter stayed with his brother's body, Soren ran for help to Clayton McCann's home out on Hwy 73 and found Clayton pouring cement for his garage floor. McCann called the county coroner, unsure of what to do. Clayton and Soren took Clayton's car to let Soren's wife and parents, the Larson's, know what happened and then drove back to Clayton's house to wait for the coroner.

It was about 4:30 in the afternoon when the accident occurred. Eventually, Clark County Sheriff Hal Richardson and the District Attorney from the county found their way to the scene in the near darkness. The Sheriff questioned everyone and then picked up Buster's gun lying near the body, neither of which had been moved. Everyone was certain beyond a doubt that Buster started out hunting that day with just 5 shells, including Buster's wife. The Sheriff couldn't quite figure out how to unload Buster's gun, a 30-30 rifle, so Clayton McCann told him the best way would probably be to fire it in the air. McCann pulled the trigger, a shot rang out, and then he ejected the remainder of the shells from the chamber. There were still four shells left in the gun so they felt certain that Buster's gun was not the one that had caused his death.

Walter had a 12 gauge shotgun. They found it in the creek but were not able to locate the bullets he had thrown away. Walter explained that when the accident occurred he immediately threw his gun, feeling as though he never wanted anything to do with hunting again. An inquest was held at the courthouse in Neillsville three days after the accident after an examination of the body had been completed by Dr. Housely from Neillsville. It was believed after studying the evidence, the bullet that killed Buster came from a rifle, not a shotgun, and that it entered his neck, creating a small hole through his upturned shirt collar from his back side, then exited through his cheek.

A few other hunters were located and questioned at the inquest that were in the area at the time of the shooting. No one was arrested and the mystery of Buster's death was never solved.

Buster Larson, 28, was a farmer and milk hauler. He lived in the Town of Washburn and was town clerk for three years before his death. His parents, Mr. and Mrs. Ole P. Larson, lived in Sherwood when the accident took place. Buster was survived by a wife and young son.

Despite its dangers before the days of blaze orange and hunter safety courses, deer gun season was very important to the livelihood of the Sherwood community. Not only did hunting provide meat for the table but the season created more income in its short duration for local businesses than any other time of the year. The Sherwood Store took in hunters and charged them $1.00 a day in the 1940s, a fee that included home cooked meals. A breakfast was served well before daylight each morning and hunters returned to the store for dinner as well.

There have been several deer camp clubs from Sherwood through the years. One group was called "Buck & Bull". In the 1970s, B & B decided to release a brown goat with horns into the woods on opening morning, just for fun. A young hunter from Illinois was hunting in the "Square" south of the Scholtz farm when he spotted the critter and fired a perfect shot. A seasoned hunter named Ozzie, who spent a lifetime working in a meat packing plant in Iowa, and another hunter in his 30s had a heck of a time trying to help the young hunter get the metal tag on the goat. They figured since it was brown and had horns it was good enough. The goat later appeared, fully gutted out, hanging in the Scholtz barn with the other deer harvested that day. Ralph Scholtz told the hunters he'd lived there all his life and never saw a goat in the woods before. Ralph said perhaps they all had too much to drink.

Local taverns through the years and yet today pack their parking lots full when deer gun season arrives. The whitetail deer will hopefully always be there for us to enjoy with the annual deer season a time for tradition, family, and friends to gather together. It's just a big part of Sherwood and for many, deer hunting is a way of life.

Sherwood Deer Hunters – Oscar Brinkmeier's Place, North side of Hwy 73, west of the Audubon school house – L to R: Oscar Brinkmeier, Frank Sholtz, unknown (Author's Photo)

Edith (Sparks) Todd & Bert Todd on Todd Road
(Todd Family Photo)

Hunters at Charles Schwanebeck's Farm – Back Row L to R: ?, Ivan Schwanebeck, Al Schmidt, ?, ?, Charles Schwanebeck, ?, ? Front Row L to R: ?, Wayne Schwanebeck, ?, ? (Schwanebeck Family Photo)

Real Characters

A phrase I often heard as a child and that made an impression on me was to hear someone called a "real character". So, what does that mean? I guess it means they stood out over the rest of the crowd and perhaps did something unusual or a bit unexpected. Sherwood has had many real characters. Below are just a few of them who have passed on and shouldn't be forgotten. Frank Dartt, the bear trapper, has already been mentioned but would surely fit this category as would Tom La Flesh and several others previously mentioned but here are a few more "real characters" that lived in Sherwood.

NATHAN CARL LUSTER lived on the northwest side of the township from at least 1915 to 1920. Nathan Carl and his wife, Louise Luster, had three children while living in Sherwood and lost a young son. Carl, as he preferred to be called in the show business world, was a real character because of the various occupations he hoped to succeed at. A family descendant said he was always trying to be something he wasn't.

Nathan listed his occupation on each of his three children's birth records while living in Sherwood as an actor, contortionist/acrobat, and a theatrical performer. He did acrobatic acts for the circus and dabbled in vaudeville shows. At the time the family lived in Sherwood, Nathan may have worked for the Barnum & Bailey Circus at Baraboo.

Nathan married Louise Kolb at Chicago in 1914, before coming to Sherwood and when the family left, they moved back to Chicago in the mid to late 1920s. Nathan's great granddaughter said he could do tricks such as stand on two horses' backs with a third horse in between them. He also walked tightropes without a net and allowed himself to be shot out of a cannon. Nathan was a tall man. Nathan also did shows later in life, with Charley Chaplin, Milton Berle, and Sophie Tucker, traveling to California and the Palace Theatre in New York City. He was not the norm and why he chose to live in Sherwood for a short time is a mystery. Perhaps he gave contortionist acts at the Sherwood Town Hall!

ELIZABETH SPARKS ST. GERMAIN moved to Sherwood in the 1870s with her father, James Freeman Sparks. She was widowed from her first marriage, divorced from her second husband, and had two children, David Sparks, and Ascenith Sparks Lawson, wife of Andrew Lawson. David Sparks helped build the logging dam on Tom's Creek in 1880 and told his grandson that a crew of men dug dirt up by hand with shovels and used oxen to haul it to site of the dike. David later farmed in the town of Cary.

In 1880, Elizabeth married another widower, David St. Germain, and together they made their home and farm in Section 8. In 1983, M. Ward Wilson wrote a letter to Mildred Lawson, daughter-in-law of Andrew Lawson, and mentioned Elizabeth, *"She was called Aunt Lib. They lived on a farm on now Highway 73, a short distance west of "W". Had a nice 1 ½ story house... Aunt Lib was "quite a girl". She smoked a pipe, when any of the smoking boys appeared she would ask them what kind of tobacco they had. Would take a pipeful, sit in front of the stove, and smoke."* Elizabeth was taken to the Wood County Asylum in her later years and died there in 1922. People thought she went crazy but most likely this poor, kind soul suffered from dementia.

WALTER HANSON was born in Denmark in 1893. He lived in Rock County, Wisconsin, with his mother, brother and sister-in-law, when he entered the service during WWI. In the fall of 1935, Walter found himself in Sherwood, busy digging a cellar for a log home he intended to build before winter took hold, on his recently purchased forty acres. His cabin was on the north side of what we called the West Road, now Sherwood Road, right across from the road that led back into the Dartt place.

Why did Walter move to Sherwood? Rumors circulated that he was a bootlegger and had worked for Al Capone or that he was involved with the mafia and needed a hiding place. He farmed a little and worked for Henry Seltrecht part time according to his draft registration papers from WWII, but by then of course he was old enough that he didn't have to serve again.

Walter liked to argue about politics and religion with his neighbors every chance he got. He'd stop in and start ranting about a particular subject until most people became annoyed with him. Sometimes they'd aggravate him on purpose to get him to leave so they could get their work done. Walter would stay away for a few weeks until he calmed down and then come back to start another rant with whomever would listen.

Trading books with those who'd put up with him, was a favorite pastime for Walter. He'd stop at my aunt's house quite regularly in the wintertime and swap books with her, sometimes up to eight books at a time. I heard that Walter had a college education but I'm not sure if he did.

At Audubon School in the 1950s, children had to participate in fund raisers and at Christmas time the kids were assigned certain households to solicit. My brother, unfortunately, was delegated to visit Mr. Hansen's place. He found his way to Walter's cabin, not sure whether to knock on the front door or the back. He chose the back door which had a narrow entryway piled high with firewood on either side. As my young brother inched his way up to Walter's door his heart was beating a mile a minute, but he forced his fist to knock. The door opened and my brother started to relay his Christmas card pitch but before he could finish, Walter bolted at him. My brother scrambled out that entryway and off through the yard as fast as he could, fearing for his life.

I don't have a time frame for this story but my cousin, Lawrence Schafer, said one day Walter asked Harold Freedlund to drive him to Milwaukee, to see his sister. When they arrived at a certain street, in Milwaukee, Walter told Harold to drive really slow. He asked Harold to drop him off at a certain house number, then drive around the block and pick him back up. He didn't want Harold to wait outside the residence. When Harold came back around the block Walter was waiting to be picked up and he carried a small box that he never opened. Walter never revealed the contents of the box or spoke about it. When back in the car, he simply told Harold he was ready to go back home.

Walter had a habit in later years of sitting in a chair in his yard out near the road with a loaded gun across his lap. One time he fired a shot at my brother's car, busting a window out, as the car passed by. Others complained of the same thing and eventually Walter was carted off to the nursing home at Neillsville where he died on Christmas Day in 1975. When Walter passed away he was survived by his sister, a niece, and his Ford Maverick.

The party that bought Walter's place after his passing noted that the attic of his cabin home was filled with numerous pairs of soiled long johns hanging here and there. The kitchen table had about fifty layers of newspapers on it; presumably when one layer got dirty, another layer of newspapers was placed over top of it. Excitement occurred when a trunk was found in Walter's shed under a pile of hay, but the trunk was empty.

Lillian Ziemendorf said one of Walter's favorite quotes was, *"Convince a fool against his will, he's of the same opinion still!"*

MAX FALK lived on County Trunk Z on a farm on the west side of the road in Section 22. In the 1930s he owned 160 acres of farmland. I've only heard good things about Max and that he had an unusual sense of humor. His witty phrases captured everyone who knew him. A few quotes my family remembered Max saying were, *"You better watch out what you say around here 'cause everybody's regulated."* And, *"The papers say 'em, and I read 'em."* And the most repeated quote that Max thought up was one we still use today in our family, *"Everybody's crazy different!"*

When Max moved to America from Germany he first settled in Illinois and lost track of his overseas family. When he could no longer run his Sherwood farm he moved back to Rockford, Illinois. After Max passed away in the late 1940s his daughter learned that two of her father's brothers had been held as German prisoners of war at Camp Grant just south of Rockford, not far from where Max was living. It is sad to know that Max and his brothers never reconnected.

Max Falk and neighbor Charles Gall at Max's home in Sherwood (Scholtz Family Photo)

ROY FERGUSON moved to Sherwood from Washburn Township when he and his young wife purchased the Dartt land in the 1930s. Roy liked to trap and live off the land and made a home from the makeshift buildings Dartt left behind with his passing. Life was hard and winters were cold for the young family. The land the Fergusons purchased was landlocked and they asked the town board to help them build a road back into their place so their children could get to school easier, but the road was turned down. Ferguson and his wife left Sherwood, moving to La Crosse, where Roy got a job working as a game management pilot on the Upper Mississippi Wildlife and Fish Refuge. He was flying a small plane, attempting to raise a flock of ducks off a sluice near a refuge in North Dakota, when his plane crashed and burned. Roy and his flight companion were both killed after the plane caught on fire. Roy Ferguson was survived by his wife, Mina, and their two sons of La Crosse.

The **BOTDKE** Brothers lived in Section 23 on a farm in a small shack along County Trunk Z and they were both true characters. Louie was the youngest and outlived his brother, William. The brothers kept chickens in their house and thought nothing of it. Al Cramer said the

Bodtke's home was the only place so dirty that the flies fought to get out of it.

The house the Bodtkes lived in was given to them by Allen Freedlund and moved from the old Scharf place in Section 26. Several buildings in Sherwood were moved from place to place around the area during this timeframe.

One summer day my brothers were riding their bicycles home from Sherwood Lake in the 1950s, shirtless like they often were, when Louie Bodtke flagged them down. He handed them a pile of old white, long sleeved dress shirts, thinking the boys didn't have enough clothes to wear. Those white shirts were no longer white, but yellowed with age and beyond use, but it was the thought that counted.

GEORGE FLORENCE SR. was a kind hearted fellow who did a lot for the neighborhood, with children in mind especially. He'd dress up every Christmas as Santa Claus and he and his wife, Rose, would make up gift bags for all the Sherwood children including hard candy, peanuts, and Rose's homemade popcorn balls. In earlier days they would hand out the treats at school and in later days George would make house calls to all the neighbor kids. He had sleigh bells he'd ring outside the children's doors that made his Santa appearances seem so real. His "Ho, Ho, Ho" would fool any child into believing George was truly Santa and the fact that he knew each one by name and what they'd been up to lately, made his role even more credible.

ADELINE SCHADE moved to Sherwood from Chicago with her new husband, Alfred. She had worked as a housekeeper in Illinois when Alfred asked her to marry him. Adeline said she would, with the stipulation that he buy her a farm. Sherwood was where they found their dream home together. The Schades lived for many years in their well-kept home and yard on the east side of County Trunk Z in Section 36. Adeline, always known to me as, "Mrs. Schade", mowed the Sherwood Cemetery for years and did a wonderful job of it. She had an accent that you'd never forget and was a curious person, one time looking through my father's mailbox when he walked out to check it. She would have never taken anything, she just wanted to know what was in there.

ALVIN CRAMER was raised in Marathon and moved to Sherwood in 1955. He bought the farm he lived on in Section 35 with livestock included. Al had a lifelong love for horses and hosted the Sherwood Trail Rides in the 1950s and early 60s. He would invite a large crowd to gather at his farm and they'd all ride to the Sherwood Park and on toward the Sherwood Bluff. Folks came from as far away as Cataract and Marathon to attend the event, most bringing their own horses. On one trail ride a horse lay down in the creek along the trail and wouldn't get up.

The Cramer Trail Ride was an annual event that included a meal for all back at the farm with help from Al's wife, Lydia (Spaete) Cramer. Horse trading was Al's specialty. He travelled far and wide and made friends throughout the Midwest while dealing, auctioning, and looking for the right horse.

Trail Ride at the Al & Lydia Cramer Farm – 1961
Al Cramer and Al Spaete in the Lead (Schwanebeck Family Photo)

LOUIE PAUN was a man that everyone loved, with a kind heart. When younger he was always inventing things and working on patents, like a special wagon hitch. I didn't meet Louie until he was completely blind, from diabetes, but I was fascinated with the things he could do with his mind and his hands, without sight. He was mechanically minded and knew all about car engines. We had a car that had the habit of missing quite a bit. Louie would take an empty pop bottle full of water and pour it down the carburetor while we revved up the engine with a foot on the gas pedal. Never fail, his method would take care of that miss.

My husband and I were looking for a dump truck to build our driveway with when we first married. We found an old 1942 Diamond T flatbed truck with a hoist on it advertised at an auction and decided to see if Louie would come along with us and check it out. When we got to the sale, the truck was sitting abandoned in an overgrown hayfield and I thought it was nothing we'd ever consider bidding on. Well Louie put on his coveralls and crawled under that truck and felt everything from back to front and under the hood, and he said it was a good one. We ended up buying that Diamond T and it turned out to be a real special truck for us, thanks to Louie.

I can't imagine living with blindness at such a young age, but Louie found a way to accept it and live on, and still interact with all his friends. In fact, he died of a heart attack helping a neighbor fill his barn with hay.

HELEN SPARKS, twin sister to Hazel, was born in 1900, and raised in Sherwood Township. Neither Helen nor her sister ever married. Helen chose to become a school teacher early on and served the Sherwood Community so well. In her later years she cared for her sister, Hazel, and looked out for her brother Danny Sparks, who lived at Owen. Helen lived on a farm that she inherited from her parents, Jesse and Laura (Messing) Sparks. She taught school in several locations but most familiarly at Audubon School in Sherwood. Many students learned all that was necessary to carry them on through life in her 1st through 8th grade one room school settings. Helen was also active with the Sherwood Community Church and was kind to the neighborhood children. She would ask them to help do yard work and chores occasionally and give them money and treats when she knew they needed a boost.

Helen drove a beautiful 1950s Ford that was black and cream, and had a lot of chrome. She was so short she needed a lift on the gas and the brake pedals. Helen always wore dresses with lace collars and rich fabrics; she was a neat and tidy lady and an immaculate housekeeper. I'd like Helen to be remembered for all she gave back to the children of Sherwood years ago.

Recent Times

In 1974, Sherwood Township celebrated its 100th anniversary at Sherwood Park with a two day affair. Alfred Schade, 95, was honored as the oldest resident of the town. Eleanor Coulthard was the centennial chairperson and town officers; Norman Freedlund, Lois Freedlund, Milden Schwanebeck, and Alfred Fields, all helped to make the weekend special. Many Sherwood residents and past residents participated in the event.

If we began in 1975, on the northwest side of the township, and drove around ending up in the southeast part of Sherwood near the Clark/Jackson County line we would have found these names on the mailboxes: Lifto, Tison, Pederson, Rosandich, Prior, Paun, Steinwagner, Prewitt, Babcock, Scholtz, Friedrichsen, Mueller, Todd, Hutchison, Minor, Luther, Ziemendorf, Lawton, Coulthard, Moeller, Fluegel, Rojicek, Schafer, Florence, Turville, Schwanebeck, Freedlund, Jacobson, Schade, and Cramer. Today, forty years later, many of the same surnames are still found in Sherwood.

When I think hard about what the most obvious change in Sherwood's later years might be, the first thing that comes to mind is the decline of the dairy farmer. We've went from over fifty active farms in the 1940s to only two remaining dairy farms as I write this today. Farm fields are rented out to others and some have been replanted with trees once again. Will farming come back with another cycle of change in the future? That remains to be seen.

Another change that I've noticed in my lifetime is the difference in wildlife today from when I was young. We now have an abundance of turkeys in Sherwood, something unheard of fifty years ago. Bobcats and fishers make their way across the town and leave their tracks for us to see. And we also have a resurgence of timber wolves, a very controversial subject today. The bald eagles are returning too and we've even had a few whooping cranes land in Sherwood fields along with flocks of Sandhill cranes. There are a few nesting pairs of bald eagles in the area and it is not uncommon to see one along the roadside making a meal of a fresh car killed deer. Another creature that I don't welcome and didn't see much of fifty years ago is the deer tick, which has become a real problem, affecting many Sherwood household members with Lyme disease. It makes me wonder what the next fifty years will bring, and I hope it's all good.

We're down to one church and one tavern and very few children riding the school bus today in Sherwood. There are no schools and no post offices anymore. In some ways, Sherwood is a quieter community than it was years ago, but there's no doubt it's still a beautiful and peaceful place to live and to visit.

An Autumn Woods Trail off Todd Road in Sherwood

CREDITS

Excerpts from *Mary Serena La Flesh's Chronicle* shared by the La Flesh family; *Myron Pickering's Memoirs* shared by Dorothy Pickering Bullington; Elery Messing's letters from *Roselyn's Story* shared by Shelley Toutenhoofd. Letters from Axel Moeller, Cecil Moeller, David St. Germain, Helen Seman. Elsie Fluegel's Remembrances; M. Ward Wilson's Remembrances.

Interviews with Donald Freedlund via Sarah Freedlund; Lawrence Schafer; Ronald Finnestad; Carol Blattler; Lydia Cramer; Anna Martin; Lillian Ziemendorf; Theresa Mallory; Marla Martin; Frances Ziemendorf; Dixie Jacobson; Lillian Ziemendorf; Shannon Luster; Paula Schafer; Lynn Moeller; Sharon Steinwagner; Paula Schafer.

Photos from *The Fields Collection* – Wilbur & Elsie Fields; Jennifer Shirk; Dorothy Pickering; Jack La Flesh; Carol Blattler; Schwanebeck Family; Jacobson Family; Freedlund Family; Moeller Family; Scholtz Family; Schafer Family; Brinkmeier Family; Ziemendorf Family; Carin Schalla; Luther Family; Fluegel Family; Schafer Family.

News articles from: *Neillsville Republican & Press*; *Neillsville Press*; *Evening Star* of La Crosse; *Pittsville Record, Republican and Leader* of La Crosse

Special thanks to Paula Schafer, Neda Johnson, Sarah Freedlund, and Marla & Ron Martin for help with editing and my husband, Tom, for inspiring me to write this history.

Thanks to everyone, those living and those passed, who have shared their family history, stories, photos, and memories with me.

Kay Scholtz